ETERNAL REWARDS

IT WILL PAY TO OBEY

By Lucas Kitchen

To view the free companion videos for this study go to

SIMPLYBELIEF.COM/REWARDS

TABLE OF CONTENTS

THE PREPARATION FOR VICTORY

CHAPTER 1

When I was in fourth grade, I asked my Dad if I could get into baseball. I had seen a game or two on TV and liked the look of the sport. I imagined that the entire experience would consist of a crisp uniform, a few Saturday morning games, and a big trophy. I was surprised to find that there were all kinds of tasks that had to be done before we even had one game.

I was expected to play catch with Dad each evening to prepare for what would happen at practice. There were about thirty scheduled practices a week, at least that's what it felt like. We ran laps over and over. We had to learn a list of terms and rules. We were encouraged to do extra batting practice. I

To view the video for this chapter
GO TO **SIMPLYBELIEF.COM/ER1**
Or scan the QR code with phone camera.

was even instructed to oil my glove each night before I went to bed. I had expected wild fun. What I got was hard work.

We won a few games that year, only because we spent a lot of time preparing. The teams that beat us had obviously spent more time preparing.

Almost anything you do in life has a phase like this: practices, rehearsals, and run-throughs required before the final contest. If you want to succeed, you have to ready yourself for the big event. Did you know that the same is true for those who want to win spiritual victory?

This book is for those who are already believers. If you've recently become a Christian or even if you are a long-time Christ follower, you have a big season ahead of you. There is some preparation work that you need to do for the championship match that you're facing.

The first major section of this book is called "Preparation for Victory." It is devoted to laying out the playbook and getting a fix on the basics so that you are ready to play for the win. Our team's secret weapon is what we call "Eternal Rewards." More on that in a while. For now, it's time to get ready. Maybe say a little prayer to get your heart in the right place. Once you've done that, turn the page both in this book and in your life. What we're going to learn will change your life if you let it.

Some will be

GREAT

While others will be

LEAST

In the Kingdom of Heaven.

A believer's greatness in Heaven will be based on their
OBEDIENCE TO CHRIST ON EARTH.
Matthew 5:19

THE DISCOVERY
CHAPTER 2

I grew up in a Bible-teaching church. We learned the Bible verse by verse. It was an incredible, almost seminary level, biblical education. In my early twenties, I branched out and worked in various ministry capacities in churches of all sizes. I minored in biblical studies in undergrad and majored in biblical studies in seminary. I traveled doing music ministry for about a decade with a host of speakers and evangelists. From the time I could understand speech until I was 30, I estimate that I heard over 10,000 talks on biblical subjects. That's thousands of sermons, Bible studies, discussions, and lectures. This doesn't count the stack of books I've read concerning biblical topics. You might expect after all of that biblical training that I would have been well versed in the concept of reward in Heaven. However, if you think that,

To view the video for this chapter GO TO **SIMPLYBELIEF.COM/ER2** Or scan the QR code with phone camera.

you'd be wrong.

Out of those 10,000 sermons, lectures, and Bible studies, there was almost never a mention of reward in Heaven as distinct from salvation. I remember one sermon when I was in junior high on the subject of rewards in Heaven. That's it. Now before you assume I was snoozing, think again. I am a listener. I've been paying attention to what people are saying about the Bible all my life. Nonetheless, there was one sermon on the subject that I can remember. It came from the book of Hebrews. These years passed me by with almost no mention of the concept that there would be a reward above and beyond salvation for those who obey God.

In my early thirties, I was challenged on this topic. I began to attend a church that taught on the subject. I was skeptical at first. I assumed there might be only a few references to reward in Heaven in the Bible. I thought this since it was a subject so few Bible teachers taught. After all, I was no novice regarding biblical topics. How could I have gone through thirty years of intensive Bible training and missed something so fundamental? It was nearly impossible for me to believe that I had never heard of something so essential to the Christian life. I began to do some research. Then more research. Later more still. What I found came as such a surprise.

I found reference after reference to *reward in Heaven*. As I expanded my search, I discovered that the concept is talked about, often under many different terms. These terms could not be synonyms for salvation for various reasons. I was faced with a paradigm shift. This simple thesis began to bloom in my mind:

> Not everyone will be equal in Heaven because some
> Christians will gain reward for their obedience on

earth while others will miss out on reward because of their disobedience on earth.

I was faced with a dilemma. Either I could cling to the old mindset, that everyone gets the same reception, recognition, and reward in Heaven, or I could jettison that faulty idea for what I actually found in the Bible. Think of this famous phrase of Jesus:

> Do not think that I came to destroy the Law or the Prophets... Whoever therefore breaks one of the least of these commandments, and teaches men so, shall be called least in the kingdom of Heaven; but whoever does and teaches *them*, he shall be called great in the kingdom of Heaven.

This verse and many others show that there are those who will have different status in Heaven. I reluctantly began to rearrange the wreckage of 30 years of Bible training. I let the word of God begin to change my thinking on the subject, and I've not looked back.

As I began to do research for this project, I thought it would be valuable to see how many of the books of the New Testament talk about working for eternal rewards. Once again I was aghast. On a warm spring afternoon, I began my search. Page after page I dug for the treasure I was after, though, the gold was not buried deep. I found direct references to eternal reward in 24 of the 27 books of the New Testament. That was enough to be convinced of the importance, but I wanted more. I scoured the remaining three books to see if there were any short references to working for eternal rewards. After just one reading each, I discovered what I was looking for. I was not as surprised this time to find that they did, in fact, discuss the idea with a few brief statements.

Now think about this for a second. I'm claiming that every New Testament author talks about eternal rewards. Every. Single. One. When they speak about eternal rewards, they are not discussing salvation, but instead a bonus, an extra payout, a reimbursement in Heaven for work done on earth. Not only does every author mention it, but every book in the New Testament discusses the idea that Christians who have the free gift of salvation should then be working for eternal reward in Heaven. Believers are not forced to work for rewards; they are invited. Some take up the banner and live like lions among kittens. Others, not so much.

Are you like I was? Have you missed this fundamental theme in the Bible? If so, that's ok. It's never too late to learn. Maybe you've heard of rewards, but never grasped the gravity of the subject. I sincerely hope today is the day. I believe there is no better method for sustained victory in the Christian life. If you want the power to overcome this life and the troubles it comes with, the answer is rewards.

Now, I'd like to share with you what I found. I am providing the lists in the following pages as a quick guide to help you see how often and how thorough the Bible is concerning eternal rewards. Two reference tools are included: the first is a list of the terminology used to describe rewards in the Bible. The second is a concise list by books of the Bible showing the significant passages about eternal rewards. This list certainly doesn't contain every reference to eternal rewards in the New Testament, but is a reasonably thorough study for further reading. These lists will act as unique tools in your journey of discovery. You may choose to quickly scan the listings, or study them in depth. Either way is fine, though the rest of the book will be devoted to discussing verses that appear on these lists. Enjoy!

REWARDS
TERMINOLOGY
AND REFERENCES

REWARDS
TERMINOLOGY
Here are some terms the Bible uses to describe rewards in Heaven.

 REWARD IN HEAVEN

 PRIZE

 GOD'S PRAISE GLORY AND HONOR

 FRUIT OR HARVEST

 WAGES

 RULERSHIP OR REIGN

 REPAYMENT

INHERITANCE

 TREASURE IN HEAVEN

 CROWNS

 PROFIT

 BETTER RESURRECTION

 RICH WELCOME INTO THE KINGDOM

 HIDDEN MANNA AND WHITE STONE

 MORNING STAR

 WHITE GARMENTS

REWARDS &
REFERENCES

Here are some biblical references to various rewards in Heaven.

MATTHEW

Inherit 5:5
Reward 5:12, 46, 6:1-6, 16-18, 10:41-42, 16:24-27
Treasure 6:19-21, 19:21
Thrones 19:27-28
Right Hand Seat 20:23
Ruler 25:14-30

MARK

Reward 9:41
Treasure 10:21

LUKE

Reward 6:23, 35
Repaid 14:14
Treasure 12:33-34, 18:22
Authority 19:11-27

JOHN

Fruit 4:35-36
Honor 12:26
Abundant life 10:10
A place for you 14:2
Praise of God 12:42-43

ACTS

Inheritance 20:32, 26:28

ROMANS

Repay 2:6,
Heirs 8:17-18

1 CORINTHIANS

Reward 3:8-15, 9:24-27
Inherit 6:9-10
Crown 9:25
Praise from God 4:2-5

2 CORINTHIANS

Receive what is due 5:10

GALATIANS

Inherit 5:21
Reap 6:6-10

EPHESIANS

Reward 6:8
Inheritance 1:14, 18, 5:5

PHILIPPIANS

Prize 3:12-14
Fruit 4:15-17

COLOSSIANS

Reward 3:24-25
Inheritance 1:12, 3:24

1 THESSALONIANS

Crown 2:19
Blameless 3:13, 5:23

1 TIMOTHY

Treasure 6:18-19

2 TIMOTHY

Crown 2:5-6, 4:7-8
With eternal glory 2:10
Reign with Him 2:12

TITUS

Heirs 3:7

HEBREWS

Reward 10:34-35, 11:6, 24-26,
Inherit 6:10-12,
Better resurrection 11:35

JAMES

Crown 1:12
Inherit 2:5
Mercy 2:13

1 PETER

Crown 5:4
Inheritance 1:4, 3:9
Honor 1:6-7

2 PETER

Rich welcome 1:10-11

1 JOHN

Confidence 2:28
Boldness 4:17

2 JOHN

Rewarded 1:8

JUDE

Exceeding Joy 1:24

REVELATION

Crown 2:10, 3:11
Reward 22:12
Repay 2:23
Inherit 21:7
Manna and stone 2:17
Power over nations 2:26-27
Morning star 2:28
Clothed in white 3:5

MOTIVATED
CHAPTER 3

Everyone needs motivation. It's an essential function of the human brain. Everyone needs to see what the payout will be for their trouble. You work for a paycheck, not for free. You work out at the gym for a purpose, to lose weight. You take a shower every once in a while because it benefits your social life. There is a motive for everything. Every beat of your heart and breath in your chest has a motive.

God designed you. You know that, right? He designed you to be motivated by incentives. He encoded your elaborate DNA to expect a payout, a consequence, an equal and opposite reaction. He built nature such that those without motivation can never win. Winners are motivated. Champions have passion. Victors have incentives.

Take away the incentives, and the winners will find another sport. Give everyone a trophy just for being present, and the

To view the video for this chapter
GO TO **SIMPLYBELIEF.COM/ER3**
Or scan the QR code with phone camera.

talent will dry up. But if you make the reward a million bucks, everyone will want to play. And they'll play hard. Action and motivation are married, and it's not one of those awkward marriages where you know they don't even like each other. Action and motivation are so closely related, you can't pry them apart.

If you've believed in Jesus for salvation, then congratulations. Your eternal home is guaranteed, but your success as a disciple is not. You will either be a winner or a loser concerning the Christian life. Being a loser at the sport of discipleship won't jeopardize your salvation; but it has its consequences, and they're a real kick in the gut.

What's the difference between Christian winners and losers? Motivation. Those who understand what's at stake are a quadrillion times more likely to be Christian winners. No, the word quadrillion is not in the Bible, not even in the message, though the concept I'm talking about is.

You will either be a Christian success because you have the motivation to fight for the win or you will be Christian failure. If you wind up as a Christian failure, you will enter Heaven as such. You'll have to explain why you wasted your life. Jesus will acknowledge that you really "smooched the pooch" on this one. You'll then have to live out your eternal existence in Heaven knowing that you failed at the first task of eternity, your mortal life. Motivation is paramount to your spiritual success.

God offers incentives for anyone who wants to attempt being a good disciple. I'm not talking about eternal life or salvation here. That's a free gift. I'm talking about benefits above and beyond salvation. I'm talking about some real bankroll. This isn't some E for effort nonsense. This is the big leagues, and they play for keeps. The trophy for this sport is Grade A eternal. You have before you either shame or glory.

You choose by every step you take, every move you make.

Before we examine rewards that we will experience in eternity, let's talk about the here-and-now rewards which are available for those who live out their faith.

There are lots of physical consequences for abandoning and rewards for living out your faith. For instance, porn addiction will wreck your sex life (with your spouse). Having a sex life without a spouse can give you SDIs. Gluttony will destroy your health. Violence will land you in jail. Slander will get you punched. I'm sure you get the idea. Sin damages lives. Living a godly life is rewarding. There is a better quality of life now waiting for those who abandon sin and live for Christ.

There are also mental rewards which come with living a life of discipleship. God included a moral compass with our mental map. We have an innate sense of right and wrong. When we leave the path marked out on that mental map, it causes internal tension, dissatisfaction, frustration, and mental fog. That's why living an ethical life is mentally rewarding. Personal and moral satisfaction is a here-and-now reward that a committed disciple can experience. Those who fight to live out their faith can experience a powerful internal gratification and ease that mental turmoil.

Social rewards are probably the most potent present incentive for Christian living for believers. Maybe it's because you're afraid the church ladies will look down their powdered noses from their upholstered pew at you. Perhaps it's because you love the Christian camaraderie you get from your congregation. Whatever the reason, we are designed to find community comforting and rewarding. The social benefit that comes from living a life of faith is enormous.

Spiritual rewards are all about your relationship with God. Many people report that what motivates them to keep the faith is a desire to please God. Others say that they are driven to live out the Christian life because of gratitude to God for salvation. These are some spiritual motivations for godly action.

We've talked about physical, mental, social, and spiritual rewards that committed disciples can experience here-and-now. Many believers find these present rewards of a Christian life enough to stay on the straight and narrow. That is plenty for some, but I have to be honest. These motivations have their limits. They are not bad or wrong, but if we rely only on these here-and-now motivations, we will likely hit a wall. There's only so much you will be willing to sacrifice if the only motivation you are aware of is in the here-and-now. Let's consider the limitations of these present rewards.

Present physical rewards have worked to keep me from hard drink, promiscuous sex, and other life-ruining sins. However, in my twenties I didn't think that porn could possibly wreck my life so, game on! I found it physically rewarding to avoid the so-called "big" sins. I didn't smoke crack because it would fry my brain, and I didn't do meth because it would rot my teeth— I'm very fond of my teeth. However, I developed quite a potty mouth and talked badly about people behind their backs. Present physical rewards can help us stay away from the dangerous habits, but they are often too weak a motivator to fine-tune our Christian life.

Present mental rewards have their place as well. For a time after college, I distanced myself from other Christians. I had become complacent in my porn consumption and even had begun to justify it. That caused a lot of bitterness, frustration, and mental fog. The storm that was starting to blow in my mind was a red sky warning that I needed to course correct. The moral tension I felt was an internal pressure for me to move back to the light. The here-and-now consequence of mental dissatisfaction acted as a warning signal, but it was not powerful enough to motivate me to mount a serious battle against my sin. The reward of mental peace was something I wanted, but that desire wasn't strong enough to make me leave porn behind.

Present social rewards have helped me live out my faith as long as I've stayed close with other godly Christians and been honest. However, there have been times when I just pretended like my heart was in it. At times, I found myself isolating from Christian friends, which dulled the social reward I got from being in a community of faith. That is one of the weaknesses of here-and-now social rewards: and they don't always work if you're not honest and they don't work for those who are isolated.

Present spiritual rewards like closeness with God can work to keep us on the straight and narrow, sometimes. The problem for me at that point in my life was I liked pleasing myself. I mean I *really* liked it. I spent my money however I wanted. I watched any kind of X-rated garbage I liked. I cussed people out behind their backs. I had bursts of anger, which was negatively affecting my wife. When I was around Christians, I pretended to be a well-behaved believer, but I knew the truth. I would hear people talk about how rewarding it is to be in close fellowship with the Creator, but I found it rewarding enough to pursue my own desires and interests.

All of this led to dark waters and stormy skies. My boat was pitching in the gale, and I didn't know what to do about it. I was living life my way, and *my approach* was getting more raunchy by the day. The here-and-now rewards I knew about weren't powerful enough to overcome my private desires. Here-and-now consequences were enough to keep me from becoming a murderer or a rapist. They kept me from going off the deep end, but they weren't enough to get me out of the shallow water. I was acting like none of it mattered, and I could feel my life taking on water fast.

Through those years what I kept running into was this:

> "I know I'm saved, so why should I try to live like a saint? It's tough."

The answer eventually came, and things began to change. The change was not easy. It was and still is hard work. In the following years, I began and am still working on the areas that I mentioned before. I turned digital authority over to my wife. I had her put a passcode on all our devices so that I can't watch anything rated R or worse, without her knowing. I continue to work on my language and how I talk about others. I've made progress in ways that would have surprised me a few years ago. I have to stay vigilant, but I'm excited about the changes.

So the question you should be asking is… Come on, you know it. What is the obvious question? The obvious question is, "What motivated the change." The change came when I learned something. It was something pretty simple. It was something I should have known, but I didn't. I learned about a fundamental truth that is woven throughout the Bible, but I had never heard discussed.

The motivation that I needed came when I was taught about eternal rewards. Eternal reward is not the same thing as salvation. (More on that in the next sections.) Eternal reward offers an incentive to do as Christ commands. If you accept the concept of here-and-now rewards, which we have been talking about, you can think of eternal reward as an extension which will stretch into eternity. I'm quite confident that once you understand this concept, it will provide you the motivation you need to pick up your weapon and fight. That's not only because I've seen it work in my life, but because I've seen it work in others' lives as well. Here is a chart. I like charts. I like this chart. You should too.

MOTIVATION FOR CHRISTIAN LIVING		
TYPE	PRESENT REWARDS	ETERNAL REWARDS
Physical	Better Quality Of Life	Better Eternal Life
Mental	Joy and Peace	More Satisfaction
Social	Enhanced Relationships	Serve Others More
Spiritual	Closeness To God	Closer To God

Eternal Physical Reward: If you stay committed to doing good works, you can experience a higher quality of eternal life than someone who is saved but lives like the devil. There are actual physical benefits in Heaven that not everyone will experience, only those who stay faithful.

Eternal Mental Reward: A fuller satisfaction available is available in Heaven for those who do the hard work of discipleship here. It's a more complete joy that won't be available for those who went dormant during their mortal life.

Eternal Social Reward: Those who work for Christ until the end of their lives will be given more opportunity in Heaven to serve others through leadership. The social aspects of Heaven are fantastic, especially for those who are trustworthy disciples now.

Eternal Spiritual Reward: The most significant incentive for godly living is a closer eternal relationship with God and Christ. Not everyone's relationship with Jesus will be the same in Heaven. Some will sit at his right and left hand, while others will not have such a close interaction.

Maybe you feel beaten down. Perhaps you're not excited about your faith. Maybe you've considered giving up altogether. I believe as we look at what the Bible has to say about eternal rewards, you will find the strength to step back into the ring and box like a champ until the final bell has rung. Stick with me; I'm going to teach you how to fight.

THE DIFFERENCE
CHAPTER 4

To view the video for this chapter
GO TO **SIMPLYBELIEF.COM/ER4**
Or scan the QR code with phone camera.

What is a reward? Think of that moment when you're handed your paycheck after a long month of labor, or that championship trophy your team won. Even the diploma you received at the end of a difficult education is a reward. Reward is a thing given in exchange for one's service, effort, or achievement. Our lives are built on a cycle of work and reward. Almost everything we do has some component of this process.

It's for that reason that we must not confuse a reward with a gift. A gift is something given to someone without any payment in return. A birthday present, a charitable donation, or a family inheritance are examples of gifts. You don't have to work to receive this kind of present. Do you see the difference? It's imperative that you do. A birthday present and a paycheck are two very different things. The difference between a gift and a reward is an excellent analogy for the difference between eternal life and eternal rewards.

Eternal life is not an eternal reward since you receive eternal life for free. Eternal reward is not a free gift since you will have to work to earn that reward. Eternal life is given to anyone who believes in Jesus.[1] Eternal life, sometimes called salvation, is a free gift that cannot be earned, returned, or lost.

However, to get reward from Christ, you must work for it. Reward in Heaven is a return on your investment of obedience. Reward is a paycheck for your hard work as a disciple.[2] The following pages contain some graphical depictions of the difference between eternal life and eternal rewards.

---

1. John 3:16, 36, 5:24, 6:47, 11:24-26

2. If you are not clear on the difference between salvation and discipleship, see my previous book *Salvation and Discipleship: Is There A Difference?*

Eternal **LIFE**

Entrance into Heaven

Freely given for believing in Jesus while on Earth.

John 3:16

Eternal **REWARDS**

Extra Privileges in Heaven

Earned by obedience to God on Earth.

Revelation 2:7, 17, 26; 3:5, 12, 21; 22:14,

ETERNAL LIFE is a gift all believers currently have which will win the final victory over death.

John 5:24

ETERNAL REWARDS are the incentive God offers to motivate continued victory during this life.

1 Corinthians 9:24-25, Philippians 3:14

REWARD IS COMPENSATION

CHAPTER 5

Almost every movie in the western genre involves a wanted poster. A sandy colored page with black ink is nailed to a saloon entrance or the jailhouse wall by the local marshall. It always warns of the dangers of the criminal at large. It often includes a description of the crime committed. These are not what make wanted posters a point of common interest, though. There is one feature that makes it the talk of the town. Everyone is interested in the reward. The reward, in terms of a wanted poster, is the amount of money someone will receive if they subdue the criminal and bring him in.

If a hero is brave enough to round up the criminal, he will receive a healthy bounty for his effort. Beware, though, the bigger the reward, the more dangerous the criminal. It isn't worth it to hunt down and capture a nefarious gang boss unless the payout is substantial. No one would risk their life for nothing. No one would venture a deadly mission unless the reward makes the danger worth their while. Reward is the motivation for every bounty hunter, whether in the movies or in real life.

There's a distinction between reward and a free gift. The reward is not for just anyone who sees the poster. Asking or even begging the sheriff for the reward won't help if you haven't rounded up the bad guy. It doesn't matter how many times you've read the wanted poster, memorized the criminal's face, or told others about his actions. There is a task that must be completed to get the reward. Bringing the outlaw halfway to the jailhouse won't gain you the reward. You must bring the criminal in, completely. The reward is for a completed task.

This should help us gain a solid understanding of what reward is. To reinforce this idea, we must look at the original language of the Bible. Don't worry; I'll do the heavy lifting. We'll keep it simple. A handful of words are used in the New Testament which get translated *reward*. *Misthos,*[1] *antapodosis,*[2] *misthapodosia,*[3] and *apodidomai*[4] are the most common Greek words for *reward*.[5] None of them means *a free gift*. They all mean a repayment for some action or work done. Therefore, these words are not used to explain the free gift of salvation. They are explaining some other reality that will be present in Heaven. Some modern synonyms might be wages, reimbursement, payment, compensation, and retribution.

---

1. μισθός (misthos) is one of the Greek words that gets translated reward or wages. This word means pay or wages owed for work performed. This is the root of the Greek word that means hired worker. This word never means a free gift, but could almost always be translated for wages or payment.

2. ἀνταπόδοσις (antapodosis) means a compensating reward in repayment for some work or action. It is not a free gift.

3. μισθαποδοσία (misthapodosia) It means recompense, retribution, repayment. It can either be positive repayment, or negative repayment.

4. ἀποδίδομαι (apodidomai) to pay, implying payment of an insured obligation.

5. James Swanson, *Dictionary of Biblical Languages with Semantic Domains: Greek New Testament* (Oak Harbor: Logos Research Systems, Inc., 1997).

Like the bounty on a wanted poster, this reward is available only to those who complete the required task.

Often when a Bible verse is talking about a payment of actual money on earth for labor done on earth, the word is translated as *wages* or *pay*. However, when the verse is talking about what will be received in Heaven for good work done on earth, the translators often pick the English word *reward*. It should be remembered that the word that gets translated as *wages* or *pay* is the same word that comprises the phrase *rewards in Heaven*. Thus those who receive reward in Heaven are ones who will be getting a reimbursement, payment, or compensation for the work they've done. The work may not be easy, but that's why it will be worth it.

Most Christians have a bias toward thinking of *reward in Heaven* as *payment* because it sounds too business-like, mercenary, or even self-serving. Every time I speak about rewards, a few people in the crowd cringe a little at finding out that God plans to reimburse believers for their good work done on earth. Thus, payment, wages, salary, reimbursement, compensation, and words like these are almost completely absent from discussions about *reward in Heaven*. I don't think they should be.

Reward in Heaven is compensation that will be given to believers who do work for the Lord on earth. As you will see in later chapters *reward in Heaven* can be defined using these six categories: Riches, Recognition, Rights, Regalia, Royalty, and Relationship. There is much to unpack on the subject of reward in Heaven. First, we must clarify what reward is not.

Salvation in heaven is a free gift.

Romans 6:23

Rewards in Heaven require work on earth.

2 John 1:8

GIFTS ARE FREE, NOT EARNED.

Eternal life, the indwelling of the Holy Spirit, and everlasting citizenship in the Kingdom of Heaven

ARE ETERNAL GIFTS.

They are freely given to those who believe in Jesus.
Ephesians 2:8-9

REWARDS ARE EARNED, NOT FREE.

Eternal crowns, treasure in heaven, honor from God, and a closer relationship with Christ,

ARE ETERNAL REWARDS.

They are earned by obedience to Christ during this life.
1 Corinthians 3:8

NOT PROSPERITY
CHAPTER 6

I must issue this warning. Many people have run aground thinking that the reward that God gives is wealth in this life. Slick-haired televangelists point crooked fingers into cameras every night and make promises that Jesus never made. There are some benefits in this life when we follow Jesus, but there are as many difficulties and hurdles. So in this book when I talk about reward, I'm speaking in terms not at all similar to those of the health and wealth preachers. I'm not talking about "name it and claim it" theology. I'm not proposing a "blab it and grab it" mentality. The charlatan blabs while he grabs your money. That's not what this book is about. I am reminded of Paul's words when he said that church leaders must not be "greedy for money."[1] He didn't say this once but thrice in various letters. He knew it would become a problem,

---

1. 1 Timothy 3:8

and it still is. In another place he said:

> For the love of money is a root of all kinds of evil,
> for which some have strayed from the faith in their
> greediness, and pierced themselves through with
> many sorrows.[1]

Thus, we must make no mistake. Gaining eternal reward can't be about money in this life. It can't be about having more wealth or even more health. After all, Jesus said:

> "In the world you will have tribulation...."[2]

While you are in the world, you need to know what to expect. If you follow Jesus openly and publicly, you will encounter tribulation. You will have times of crushing pain, emotional distress, and awful opposition. When this book discusses *reward in Heaven*, we do not deny that there will be *tribulation on earth*. The reward that God gives is not health or wealth on earth. In fact, if you want reward in Heaven one of the ways to receive it is to be willing to give up on your own health and wealth and live dangerously for the kingdom until it comes.

---

1. 1 Timothy 6:10

2. John 16:33

THE FIGHT FOR VICTORY

CHAPTER 7

The following pages contain twelve practical things you can do if you are a believer. The Bible teaches that each of these things will result in receiving a reward from the Lord when you arrive in Heaven. Some of these things are easy; some will take Jedi level mastery. As a believer, you can begin today to gain eternal rewards by doing what the following pages instruct. As you go through these, spend a little time on each page considering how you may get started or improve in each area.

To view the video for this chapter
GO TO **SIMPLYBELIEF.COM/ER7**
Or scan the QR code with phone camera.

BELIEVERS WILL GET REWARDS IN HEAVEN
FOR PRAYING TO GOD ON EARTH.

MATTHEW 6:5-6 // And when you pray, you shall not be like the hypocrites. For they love to pray standing in the synagogues and on the corners of the streets, that they may be seen by men. Assuredly, I say to you, they have their reward. But you, when you pray, go into your room, and when you have shut your door, pray to your Father who is in the secret place; and your Father who sees in secret will reward you openly.

BELIEVERS WILL GET REWARDS IN HEAVEN
FOR ASSEMBLING TOGETHER ON EARTH.

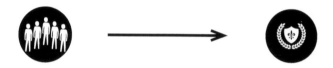

HEBREWS 10:24-25, 35 // And let us consider one another in order to stir up love and good works, not forsaking the assembling of ourselves together, as is the manner of some, but exhorting one another, and so much the more as you see the Day approaching... Therefore do not cast away your confidence, which has great reward.

BELIEVERS WILL GET REWARDS IN HEAVEN
FOR CHARITABLE GIVING ON EARTH.

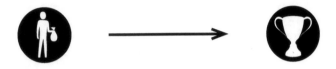

MATTHEW 6:3-4 // But when you do a charitable deed, do not let your left hand know what your right hand is doing, that your charitable deed may be in secret; and your Father who sees in secret will Himself reward you openly.

LUKE 12:33-34 // Sell what you have and give alms; provide yourselves money bags which do not grow old, a treasure in the heavens that does not fail, where no thief approaches nor moth destroys. For where your treasure is, there your heart will be also.

BELIEVERS WILL GET REWARDS IN HEAVEN
FOR SERVING OTHER BELIEVERS ON EARTH.

HEBREWS 6:9-12 // But, beloved, we are confident of better things concerning you, yes, things that accompany salvation, though we speak in this manner. For God is not unjust to forget your work and labor of love which you have shown toward His name, in that you have ministered to the saints, and do minister. And we desire that each one of you show the same diligence to the full assurance of hope until the end, that you do not become sluggish, but imitate those who through faith and patience inherit the promises.

BELIEVERS WILL GET REWARDS IN HEAVEN
FOR SHOWING KINDNESS TO THE NEEDY.

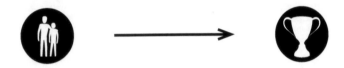

LUKE 14:12-14 // Then He also said to him who invited Him, "When you give a dinner or a supper, do not ask your friends, your brothers, your relatives, nor rich neighbors, lest they also invite you back, and you be repaid. But when you give a feast, invite the poor, the maimed, the lame, the blind. And you will be blessed, because they cannot repay you; for you shall be repaid at the resurrection of the just."

BELIEVERS WILL GET REWARDS IN HEAVEN
FOR DOING GOOD WORKS ON EARTH.

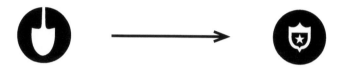

1 TIMOTHY 6:18-19 // Let them do good, that they be rich in good works, ready to give, willing to share, storing up for themselves a good foundation for the time to come, that they may lay hold on eternal life.

BELIEVERS WILL GET REWARDS IN HEAVEN
FOR RIGHTEOUSNESS ON EARTH.

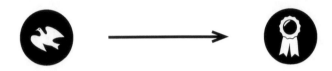

2 TIMOTHY 4:7-8 // I have fought the good fight, I have finished the race, I have kept the faith. Finally, there is laid up for me the crown of righteousness, which the Lord, the righteous Judge, will give to me on that Day, and not to me only but also to all who have loved His appearing.

BELIEVERS WILL GET REWARDS IN HEAVEN
FOR CONFESSING CHRIST ON EARTH.

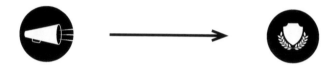

MATTHEW 10:32 // Therefore whoever confesses Me before men, him I will also confess before My Father who is in heaven.

BELIEVERS WILL GET REWARDS IN HEAVEN
FOR DOING EVANGELISM ON EARTH.

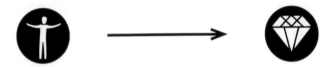

JOHN 4:35-36 // Do you not say, 'There are still four months and then comes the harvest'? Behold, I say to you, lift up your eyes and look at the fields, for they are already white for harvest! And he who reaps receives wages, and gathers fruit for eternal life, that both he who sows and he who reaps may rejoice together.

BELIEVERS WILL GET REWARDS IN HEAVEN
FOR ENDURING TRIALS ON EARTH.

JAMES 1:12 // Blessed is the man who endures temptation; for when he has been approved, he will receive the crown of life which the Lord has promised to those who love Him.

BELIEVERS WILL GET REWARDS IN HEAVEN
FOR ENDURING PERSECUTION ON EARTH.

HEBREWS 10:34-35 // For you had compassion on me in my chains, and joyfully accepted the plundering of your goods, knowing that you have a better and an enduring possession for yourselves in heaven. Therefore do not cast away your confidence, which has great reward.

HEBREWS 11:35 // ...Others were tortured, not accepting deliverance, that they might obtain a better resurrection.

BELIEVERS GET A **FULL REWARD** IN HEAVEN
FOR FAITHFULNESS UNTIL DEATH ON EARTH.

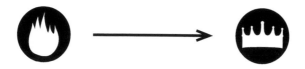

2 TIMOTHY 2:12 // If we endure, We shall also reign with Him.

2 JOHN 1:8 // Look to yourselves, that we do not lose those things we worked for, but that we may receive a full reward.

REVELATION 2:26 // And he who overcomes, and keeps My works until the end, to him I will give power over the nations.

RUN
CHAPTER 8

Athletic events were a spectacle in the ancient world. Runners removed their clothes, knee or ankle length robes, before a race in order that they not get entangled in them. The one judging the race sat at the end of the track. The runner fixed his eyes on the judge as he ran. The winner would be given a prize by the judge who sat upon a *Bema*, often translated "judgment seat." The judge had complete authority to judge the race. If one of the athletes stepped out of his lane or jumped the start, it was up to the judge to award the rightful winner.

If you've read much of the New Testament, this might sound familiar because the Apostle Paul and the writer of Hebrews used this imagery a number of times to describe what awaits those who diligently run in the race called the Christian life.

To view the video for this chapter
GO TO **SIMPLYBELIEF.COM/ER8**
Or scan the QR code with phone camera.

Think of these words of Paul:

> My only aim is to finish the race and complete the task the Lord Jesus has given me—the task of testifying to the good news of God's grace.[1]

Paul had a specific task. He used the analogy of a race to explain what that task was like. A runner can compete well in the first leg of the race but then blow it in the last half. This concept is why sports are entertaining until the very last moments. Even a game that looks like it is won can shift in an instant.

When I was in high school, our football team made it to the state play-off game. We played well and held the lead for nearly the whole game, we began to drop behind in the last quarter. The entire year's run and the state championship came down to a field goal kick. This would be the last game that most of the guys ever played. The kick veered and came shy of the goal posts. We lost the game in the last seconds, a crushing defeat.

Paul seemed to be pointing to a similar possibility. His "task" was like a race, and he needed to finish well. He didn't want to blow it in the last quarter. The task, which was testifying the good news of God's grace, could be wrecked by a lot of things. Paul was adamant about avoiding that wreckage in the last leg.

Maybe Paul was kind of a sports nut because in another place he says:

---

1. Acts 20:24

I have fought the good fight, I have finished the race,
I have kept the faith.[1]

This is the last letter that Paul ever wrote. He was in prison by this point. He knew his life was coming to an end. He could sense that his work was nearly done. His former concern that he finish his race well apparently came to fruition. His impression was that he had done the work that God had given him. He had "finished the race." What's most striking is that he had "kept the faith." If you read through Acts, it's amazing what Paul had to suffer. He kept the faith despite tremendous odds. He faced overwhelming pressure to shrink and dissolve back into the old ways of Judaism. However, he fought on. The question that arises from this is, "Why?" Why didn't he take it easy? If his eternal life was assured, why didn't he just relax and coast on into Heaven? Why did he spend his life fighting for the faith and running this tiresome race?

Paul answers that exact question in his first letter to the Corinthians:

> Do you not know that in a race all the runners run, but only one gets the prize? Run in such a way as to get the prize. Everyone who competes in the games goes into strict training. They do it to get a crown that will not last, but we do it to get a crown that will last forever.[2]

He poured out his life for this cause, not because of gratitude for his salvation, not because he felt guilty, not because he feared Hell. All those supposed motivations that preachers often give pale in comparison to Paul's reason. The reason Paul was willing to give his life to the race was

---

1. 2 Timothy 4:7
2. 1 Corinthians 9:24-25

"the prize!" He was doing it for the payoff. He was doing it because it was going to be worth it in the end. By giving us the philosophy of sports, he also gives us the motivation for Christian living, which is to be rewarded.

I love this because we can still relate even today. We compete to win. We want the prize. Millions play junior league sports in hopes of hitting the big time in the major leagues. It's a long shot for most, but for those who make it the reward is apparently worth the work. Forbes publishes the year's top-paid athletes, and the number of zeros on their salary checks is incredible. Even modern Olympic athletes win not only a medal but a sizable cash prize. Winning a gold medal or being a top contender in any sport ensures endorsement and advertising deals that bring in a healthy income. There is a lot to be gained for those who compete at the top of their sport.

Paul uses this analogy in a very precise way. He says, "Run in such a way as to get the prize." This is not talking about salvation, but a reward for Christian achievement. There is a prize waiting for those who compete at the top of their spiritual sport. The sport here is obedience to Christ, often called *discipleship*.

Paul goes on to say that athletes, "...do it to get a crown that will not last, but we do it to get a crown that will last forever." Two Greek words translate as "crown." One, *diadema*,[1] is the crown a king would wear to signify his authority and royalty. The other, *stephanos*[2], is a "crown" or garland an athlete can win for his performance.

Some kings may inherit a *diadema* crown because of their royal heredity. If it were that word used, there might be some confusion. The type of crown that Paul is talking about, the one that you can win for obedience to Christ, is a *stephanos*.

1. Swanson, *Dictionary of Biblical Languages with Semantic.*

2. Ibid.

Since Paul uses *stephanos*, a more general word which comes from "encircled," he means to say that we must work for it. This word lets us know that Paul is not talking about a prize that we receive for free. It's something we strive hard for. So, this is a reward for hard work. It's above and beyond our salvation. It's payback for our current obedience and is given in the life to come.

The author of Hebrews, who may have been Paul, says:

> Since we are surrounded by such a great cloud of witnesses, let us throw off everything that hinders and the sin that so easily entangles. And let us run with perseverance the race marked out for us, fixing our eyes on Jesus, the pioneer and perfecter of faith.[1]

To "throw off everything that hinders" is a reference to athletes who were so serious about their craft that they were willing to compete naked in order to avoid getting tangled up as they ran. Can you imagine being so committed to winning that you'd be willing to appear nude in front of thousands of spectators? That's dedication.

Notice from the verse the analogy of a great crowd who watches the race. The crowd which is present includes both spectators and previous competitors. The chapter that this verse appears in is the "hall of fame" of the faith. It speaks of the spiritual superstars of the Old Testament. It then says that those are the ones who are watching. They are a crowd of interested spectators, but they are also those we are competing against.

Any who are faithful to Christ will receive a reward, but we are in the running with all believers from all time. Each gets a fair chance to run. So you have as much opportunity

---

1. Hebrews 12:1-2

to be faithful to Christ, as Moses, Abraham, and Joseph had. Your life may be different, but you are competing in the same sport. You are running just as they did. You have the chance to be as faithful as Daniel, or Debrah, or David. That means that you have the chance to be rewarded as generously as any of these superstars. What a race. We had better be well trained. Considering all this Paul goes on to say:

> I run thus: not with uncertainty. Thus I fight: not as one who beats the air. But I discipline my body and bring it into subjection, lest, when I have preached to others, I myself should become disqualified for the prize.[1]

This verse, and especially the word "disqualified," have given many people cold sweats. It's not eternal life that Paul is concerned about being disqualified from, but the prize which he hopes to earn and receive when he arrives in Heaven. He really wants that reward. He let the motivation of winning the prize drive him forward.

He hoped that when his race was run, and he crossed the finish line, the King of Glory would place a garland on his head for his good work. Jesus, who sits on the ultimate judgment seat, is watching so much more closely than any sports judge could. He sees every step and is eager to bestow a crown on any who run in such a way as to earn it.

---

1. 1 Corinthians 9:26-27

SELFISH?

CHAPTER 9

I was riding in the passenger seat of my friend's pickup truck not too long ago. We were hauling a trailer thirty miles south of town to pick up a fridge. We were doing this as a favor for a single mom who was in a tight spot. I had volunteered to join him, but still, my friend felt bad that it was going to take up my whole evening. He began to apologize for the long drive, the inconvenience and back pain that we would endure from lifting the appliance. Without thinking, I responded with a line that I have often used when doing something unpleasant.

"I'm doing it for rewards in Heaven," I said. He smiled, but I could tell that the phrase caught his attention. I didn't simply mean it as a polite platitude or an empty cliché. I honestly meant the words I used, and it seemed that he sensed my sincerity. He spoke up after a moment of contemplation.

"I have always felt weird about that saying," he explained.

To view the video for this chapter GO TO **SIMPLYBELIEF.COM/ER9** Or scan the QR code with phone camera.

He has been a Christian as long as I have. He was raised in the church and is an active disciple. Oh, and did I mention, he is in music ministry? He went on to explain, "It just seems selfish. If I'm doing something for the payoff, is that really a good deed?"

In hindsight, I wish I had said, "You bet it's selfish, but it's the kind of selfishness God commands us to have." I took a more measured approach in the actual conversation, but in reality that is the truth. Whether seeking reward should be called selfish is up to grammarians. If it is selfish, it is the same kind of selfishness that leads a person to eat salads for the health benefit or work hard for a bonus at the end of the year or compete in sports to win a prize. It is certainly not sinful to seek the rewards God offers. There are four main reasons I know it is not sinful or immature to seek rewards in Heaven.

As we saw in the previous section, Paul was motivated by the reward, and we would call his work "good deeds." However, Paul wasn't the only one motivated by reward. Notice what is said about Moses in the New Testament.

> By faith Moses… esteemed the reproach of Christ greater riches than the treasures in Egypt; for he looked to the reward.[1]

Take special notice of the line, "for he looked to the reward." His godly actions were motivated by the promise of reward. Say it with me, "If it was good enough for Moses, it's good enough for me." Paul and Moses both were motivated by reward. They didn't shy away from hoping to be repaid for the hard work they were doing. With them as examples, we ought not be concerned that seeking the reward God gives is a sinful endeavor. For some, this is not enough. Fortunately, there is

---

1. Hebrews 11:24-26

more evidence that reward seekers are not sinning.

A second reason we should not consider seeking heavenly reward as "sinful" is that rewards *in* the Kingdom are rewards *for* the Kingdom. What does it mean that rewards are in and for the kingdom? The first idea, "in" is simple to grasp. Reward will be dispensed to believers once we have arrived in the Kingdom of Heaven. Though there are particular rewards that Christians can receive in this life, that is not the primary focus of this book. So, reward is given in the kingdom of Heaven.

Not only will reward be given *in* the kingdom of Heaven, but also *for* the kingdom of Heaven. God gave you certain spiritual gifts so that you can enhance and edify the church with them. Likewise, God will give rewards to faithful believers to enhance and edify those who live in the kingdom of Heaven. That is what I mean when I say rewards are for the kingdom. They are not for your selfish fancies. Any rewards you receive will be used to glorify God and edify others who dwell in the kingdom.

To help us see this, Paul tells us what our primary purpose in the Kingdom will be, and therefore how we will use those rewards for the good of the kingdom of Heaven.

> And God raised us up with Christ and seated us with him in the heavenly realms in Christ Jesus, in order that in the coming ages he might show the incomparable riches of his grace, expressed in his kindness to us in Christ Jesus.[1]

God will forever use us as an object lesson to edify the people of the Kingdom of Heaven. That being our purpose, we will be able to do it as effectively as possible when we employ

---

1. Ephesians 2:6-7

the rewards he's given us. It's not selfish to seek rewards which are the tools that will allow us to do work which will benefit others. By both offering us "grace" and generously rewarding us with "his kindness" we will be the active display of God's glorious generosity. Seeking rewards then is a way of filling our tool chest for the work we will do in eternity. Being rewarded greatly in Heaven makes us able to express God's glory more brightly and clearly when we get there. An example of this is when the elders around the throne lay crowns (their rewards) at Jesus' feet in worship of him.[1] Rewards are used to edify others in the Kingdom and glorify God.

A third reason why we cannot consider being motivated by rewards a sin is because Jesus commanded us to work for rewards. There are multiple examples of this, but one of my favorites is:

> Store up for yourselves treasures in Heaven, where neither moth nor rust destroys, and where thieves don't break in and steal.[2]

It is not sinful to obey Jesus. Jesus tells us to store up treasures in Heaven. Thus, it can't be a sin to think about and be motivated by treasures and rewards in Heaven.

The greatest evidence that seeking rewards should not be considered sinful comes from God's own words. Spiritual maturity drives us to be motivated by the prize since heavenly rewards are God-centered, not me-centered. Notice what God said to Abram:

---

1. Revelation 4:10

2. Matthew 6:20

"I *am* your shield, your exceedingly great reward."[1]

Despite promising him great treasures like descendants, the promise land, and blessings, God makes it clear that He Himself was and is Abram's reward. God is not only a rewarder but a reward. He is not simply a reward but an exceedingly great reward. All of those other things which God promised him were pale in comparison. Of all the rewards there are, God is the best. What does it mean to be rewarded with God? One word: fellowship.

The true reward is God. The one who is most rewarded in Heaven is the one who will most enjoy fellowship with the Father and with Christ. The one who is closest to Him in Heaven will have the greatest experience there. So seeking rewards is equivalent to seeking a closer relationship with God. After all, every heavenly reward is connected to the fellowship the rewarded shares with the rewarder.

In writing about fellowship with the Father and with Christ, the apostle John said:

> ...that you also may have fellowship with us; and truly our fellowship *is* with the Father and with His Son Jesus Christ, and these things we write to you that your joy may be full.

The one who has the closest fellowship with the Father and with Christ will have the fullest joy. This is true both on earth and in Heaven. Everyone will experience joy in the kingdom of Heaven, but those who were faithful on earth will have a greater capacity for joy there. Their joy will be more full because the primary thing that God rewards faithful followers with is Himself. Fellowship with God is the ultimate

1. Genesis 15:1

reward to which all other rewards are subordinate. So if it is selfish to want a closer fellowship with God, then count me selfish, because I want it. The, one thing you can't claim is that seeking reward is sinful.

We've seen that being motivated by reward is not sinful. The evidence that it isn't is: first, the superstars of the faith were motivated by rewards; second, rewards are for the edification of the kingdom and glorification of God; third, we are commanded store up treasures in Heaven, and fourth, because God Himself is the ultimate reward.

JUDGMENT AVOIDED

CHAPTER 10

I arrived in my best attire. The courthouse was packed with busy people buzzing from place to place. I had not spent much time in the presence of law enforcement or court officials, so the entire experience was more than a little harrowing, even though I wasn't the one on trial.

I had a very close friend who was accused of assault with a deadly weapon. It was a situation of self defense, but his lawyer convinced him to plead guilty and try for lighter sentencing. He had resisted at first, but there was more to be gained from a penitent posture than any other.

The tension in the room was palpable at every second of the trial. The witnesses took the stand and spoke terrible

---

To view the video for this chapter
GO TO **SIMPLYBELIEF.COM/ER10**
Or scan the QR code with phone camera.

things about my friend. The prosecutor ground away at every ounce of credibility he had. The judge sat and listened with emotionless attentiveness as the details were laid bare in all of their filthy nakedness.

When the proceedings were nearly concluded, it was time for my friend to stand and receive the reward for his part in the crime. The moment of sentencing had come with the not-so-distant jingle of the cold steel of waiting shackles. The knowledge that he could receive a maximum sentence of 25 years in prison sat on the courtroom like a heavy burden. It was solely up to the judge to determine the weight of his punitive duty to the state.

You could have heard a church mouse whisper as the judge quietly considered the present evidence. My friend's body was as tense as a bowstring. His counselor placed a hand on his shoulder to still his trembling. There was no confusion concerning who held the power in the room. We all knew the judge had absolute authority. With a single word, he could eradicate the next quarter century of my friend's life, or give him complete freedom. It was the most frightening real-life moment I've witnessed.

When you hear the word "judgment" what do you think of? If you're like most, judgment conjures images of tear-filled courtrooms, crushing verdicts, and calamitous sentencing. The idea of judgment is frightening. A judgment which has an eternal consequence is enough to take your breath away.

Fortunately for those who have believed in Jesus, we don't have to fear God's white throne of fiery judgment. We know this because Jesus said:

> "Most assuredly, I say to you, he who hears My word
> and believes in Him who sent Me has everlasting life,

and shall not come into judgment, but has passed from death into life."[1]

Believing in Jesus is equivalent to believing in the one who sent him.[2] That means that anyone who believes in Jesus for salvation can be confident that these three things will happen.

First, the believer presently has eternal life.

Second, the believer will not come into a judgment of condemnation at any time in the future.

Third, the believer crossed from death to life at some point in the past—the moment they first believed.

It's a beautiful promise. Jesus is so absolutely confident that salvation is a completed transaction that He explains the past, present, and future of the person who believes in Him for eternal life. For a believer who has believed at some point in the past, they have crossed from death to life. They presently have eternal life. And they will not come under condemnation in the future. Although much can be said about the verse, our focus is the promise Jesus makes pertaining to the believer's future.

The one who "believes in him... shall not come into judgment..." has a familiar ring to something Jesus previously said a few chapters earlier:

"He who believes in Him is not condemned...."[3]

The word *condemned* is the same root word for *judgment* in

---

1. John 5:24

2. John 12:44

3. John 3:18

the previous verse. It has a connotation of a negative outcome delivered by a judge. For my friend in the opening illustration, his condemnation could have been 25 years in prison. For this verse, the condemnation could be eternity in Hell. However, Jesus promises that option has been removed for those who have believed in Jesus. This is a foundational promise. Without understanding this, the gospel is impossible to comprehend. The judgment and condemnation that we avoid is one of torment and punishment. Avoiding that condemnation is the equivalent to having eternal life.

Though final condemnation before the eternal judge is something that we get to skip out on, there is a type of judgment we must all appear before. We will look at that in the next section.

On Earth every believer either

In Heaven every believer's **OBEDIENCE** is

OBEYS, OR
JOHN 14:23

STRAYS.
1 TIMOTHY 1:6, 6:10, 21

RECORDED, AND
LUKE 8:17, HEBREWS 4:13

REWARDED.
MATTHEW 16:27

In Heaven every saved person will
GIVE AN ACCOUNT
for how they spent their life.
Romans 14:10-12

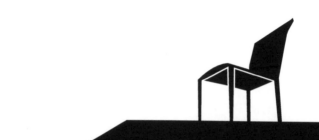

In Heaven Jesus will
GIVE THE ETERNAL REWARDS
each person earned during their life.
2 Corinthians 5:10, Revelation 22:12

LIFE APPRAISAL

CHAPTER 11

I was speaking at a small church in South Texas one summer. The church had been flooded recently and was getting a much-needed update. This meant that while I was preaching, some workers, who were not church attendees, were installing flooring in the back of the room. I don't know why they needed to do this on Sunday morning during church service hours, but I'm glad they were there. In my sermon, I was talking about the kind of judgment that Christians will have to face. Apparently, one worker was listening because in the middle of my sentence he put down his glue trowel and stood up. Seemingly unconcerned about interrupting a church service to get his inquiry answered, he interjected a loud question from the back of the room. He blurted out, "A minute ago you said Christians won't be judged, but now you're saying they will be judged. Which is it?"

This was a great question, and it gave me a good chance to offer clarification. I gestured him forward so that we could have a dialogue in front of the congregation about this important subject. What a cool guy, so eager to understand the

Bible that he would stop a sermon to find out what he wanted to know. I explained that Christians will not have to stand before the final judgment that sends people to Hell. However, there is an appraisal at which they have to appear. Though condemnation is not waiting for believers, an assessment of success is. Although eternal damnation has been taken off the table, a life-evaluation awaits those who are in Christ. We know this because Paul said:

> For we shall all stand before the judgment seat of Christ.[1]

He wrote his letter to believers in Rome. He said to those Christians that they all, including himself, will have to stand before Jesus to be assessed. Jesus' promise that we will not be condemned still stands. The judgment seat of Christ is not an event that will result in people going to Hell or any kind of condemnation. Something very different will happen there.

If our eternal destiny is set, what more is there to consider? Lots more, actually. In another place Paul says:

> We make it our aim... to be well pleasing to Him. For we must all appear before the judgment seat of Christ, that each one may receive the things done in the body, according to what he has done, whether good or bad.[2]

The judgment seat of Christ is an event that will someday require your attendance and involvement. Remember, there's no condemnation since your salvation is already in place. So, what will you do there?

He gives the answer in the same verse when he says, "that

---

1. Romans 14:10
2. 2 Corinthians 5:9-10

each one may receive the things done in the body, according to what he has done, whether good or bad."

Since you became a believer, a tally has been running. Everything you've done since that moment is being recorded. On a coming day, you will have to stand before Jesus and give a performance report. The work you've done will be weighed out and considered by the judge. The judge will then repay you for the work you've done. So it's a judgment, but it's not a judgment that has anything to do with condemnation. It has to do with performance.

Maybe it would help to remember that there are different kinds of judges. There are judges in courtrooms, but there are also judges in singing contests. There are judges for the supreme court, but there are also judges for beauty pageants. There are judges in criminal cases, but there are also judges for boxing matches. There are judges who decide penalties, but there are also judges who decide who gets the award. When he's sitting on His judgment seat, Jesus seems to be playing the role of reward giver rather than punishment dispenser.

I want to be careful here, though. Just because the judgment is not about condemnation doesn't mean it is going to be pleasant for everyone. I cannot stress this enough. You will want to be able to give a good report on that day. It would be a huge mistake for me to trivialize this event. It won't be a cakewalk for many. To see why, it might help to understand the setting.

"When and where will the Judgment Seat happen?" you might ask. Jesus answered that question with no uncertain words when He said:

> For the Son of Man will come in the glory of His Father with His angels, and then He will reward each according to his works.[1]

After Jesus was resurrected, He hung around for a little over a month, spent time with His disciples, and appeared to a bunch of people. After that, He went back to Heaven. Before He left He made a very important promise, one that we are still talking about today. He promised to return to the Earth. His return will not be like His first coming, which was humble and quiet. His second arrival will be a loud, obvious affair in which He will wrest control of the world's governments from human hands. He will conquer all the enemies that stand against him. He will change the geopolitical landscape in a single day. He will be enthroned in radiant glory on Mount Zion in Jerusalem. After all of that, He has an appointment with little ole' you. The most important and powerful person in all of history will meet with you to talk about how you did while He was out of town. Take a deep breath. It's intense.

As Paul continues with his description of what will happen at the Judgment seat of Christ, he says:

> So then each of us shall give an account of himself to God.[2]

This verse adds an emphasis that should not be missed. It places the responsibility on the one who's required to give account. Each person is accountable for his own life. You won't be able to blame your poor performance on your disobedient children. You won't get to shift the focus to an incompetent co-worker. You won't be able to wiggle out of the hot seat if your work was sub-par. You will have to give account for it. You will

1. Matthew 16:27

2. Romans 14:12

have to look the King of the world in the face and tell Him why you didn't do what He told you to do. It's going to hurt if you have been disobedient.

Now, there is a joy in this verse as well. For those who are faithful to Christ, it will be an immeasurably happy moment when they give their report. The obedient servant of Jesus will be brimming with enthusiasm as he eagerly stands before his King. The bold follower of Christ will be able to stand before the judgment seat with a confident smile, knowing that the king is not only a savior of the outcast but also a rewarder of the faithful.

So whether the Judgement Seat of Christ is a pleasant or painful event will be entirely dependent upon on how you lived. Paul adds some details to what we know about this coming event in his letter to the church of Corinth:

> Who then is Paul, and who is Apollos, but ministers through whom you believed, as the Lord gave to each one? ...and each one will receive his own reward according to his own labor.[1]

Each person has a different role to play. Paul and Apollos were both ministers. Some people in the church of Corinth considered Paul greater, whereas others considered Apollos greater. Apollos may have been a more entertaining speaker, where Paul was an academic and a theologian.[2] Paul challenges the idea by reminding them that both Paul and Apollos are just playing their part; a part that they would both be rewarded for accordingly.

In talking about himself and Apollos, Paul gives us a lesson that can be applied more broadly. He says, "Each one

---

1. 1 Corinthians 3:5-8

2. This is speculation for the purpose of illustration.

will receive his own reward according to his own labor." So even if your skill set is different from mine, the righteous judge will look deep into the life of each to determine what reward we deserve.

This leaves us wanting to know more. What will this event be like? What will be considered as we stand before the judgment seat of Christ? Fortunately, Paul does not leave us hanging. He goes on with an analogy everyone can understand. He uses a construction site as an allegory for the Judgment seat of Christ. He says:

> For we are God's fellow workers, you are God's field, you are God's building... As a wise master builder I have laid the foundation, and another builds on it. But let each one take heed how he builds on it. For no other foundation can anyone lay than that which is laid, which is Jesus Christ.[1]

He explains that there is a field on which a building is being erected. That field and building are a metaphor for the church at Corinth, and ultimately all believers everywhere. So the construction site represents the church in its various stages of growth. There are specialized construction workers that are working on this building. As in modern construction, there is a worker who specializes in foundations. That is Paul, who calls himself a master builder. The foundation represents Christ. It was Paul who introduced those in Corinth to Christ, and therefore it was he who laid the foundation.

He goes on to say there are other construction workers on the job site as well. After Paul laid the foundation, by evangelizing those there, other workers took over the project. This is where Apollos and others come in. It's not just Paul's

---

1. 1 Corinthians 3:9-11

building project, but a shared work site of all those who are part of the church. Paul then continues:

> Now if anyone builds on this foundation with gold, silver, precious stones, wood, hay, straw, each one's work will become clear; for the Day will declare it, because it will be revealed by fire; and the fire will test each one's work, of what sort it is. If anyone's work which he has built on it endures, he will receive a reward. If anyone's work is burned, he will suffer loss; but he himself will be saved, yet so as through fire.[1]

In this metaphor, Paul teaches us that the quality of our deeds will one day be tested. They will be evaluated when we stand before the Judgement Seat of Christ. All the work that we've done as a believer will be revealed, as by fire.

It's as if everything you do from the moment you become a believer is a building phase which happens on this construction site. You can build with high-quality flame-retardant, expensive materials, or you can build with dry burnable stuff you find in the yard. What you decide to build with will determine how much you are rewarded on the day you stand before Christ.

So when a Christian performs good deeds for Christ, he's building with gold, silver, and precious stones. However, when a Christian wastes time, is lazy, or neglects his discipleship, he's building with wood, hay, or straw.

One of the greatest dangers for city dwellers in the ancient world was fire. That's because so many of the houses were built with cheap flammable materials, and every home had an open flame for cooking, heating, and illumination. This metaphor would strike them at their heart since Corinth was a

---

1. 1 Corinthians 3:12-15

big city, and they had likely all witnessed house fires.

So that we can't confuse what he's talking about, Paul throws in this important final line, "If anyone's work is burned, he will suffer loss; but he himself will be saved, yet so as through fire."[1]

He's reminding us that the salvation of an individual Christian is an absolute promise even if that Christian is lazy, neglectful, and does no good deeds. Even the wicked, slothful servant[2] will be saved, but you'll smell the smoke on them when they arrive in Heaven. It's as if he's saying Christians who aren't obedient to Christ during their life will enter Heaven without a cent to their name, and their hair singed. Still, there is a reassuring promise of life for all believers whether faithful or not, but a grave warning for disobedient believers.

The verse says that the Christian who was lazy and disobedient will "suffer loss," but what does that mean? We can understand it in light of the previous verse. Paul says, "If anyone's work which he has built on it endures, he will receive a reward. If anyone's work is burned, he will suffer loss..."

So the thing in view is reward. Those Christians who work hard and stay committed will receive something very valuable. Those who are lazy and build with twigs will miss out on valuable rewards they could have had.

Can you imagine that? You could enter Heaven with a house load of gold, silver, and precious stones, or you could enter Heaven as poor as a beggar. It all depends on how you build now. If you spend every day of your Christian life seeking, obeying, and growing, you can bet you're going to be rich when you get there. If you got saved and have done nothing of spiritual value since, you may be on the path to heavenly poverty. Just like someone who has their home burnt

1. 1 Corinthians 3:15

2. Matthew 25:26

to the ground, you could suffer incredible loss if you don't get busy.

The lesson is fairly simple. As we've already seen, Paul put it so well:

Run in such a way as to get the prize.[1]

We could encircle it in all kinds of theological language, but the best metaphor for what we are to do is this:

Run!

In this chapter we've seen that once the free gift of salvation is given to the believer, no condemnation can ever befall him or her. However, everyone must go through a life-evaluation. In that accounting, our work will be assessed and judged. For those who worked hard doing the deeds, Christ commends there will be reward. For those who were lazy, there will be loss.

---

1. 1 Corinthians 9:24-25

PLEASING GOD

CHAPTER 12

I've encountered a number of people who say they are not interested in eternal rewards; they just want to please God. That's really ironic. It's ironic because it's impossible to please God or get close to Him without believing in and seeking the rewards He offers. The writer of Hebrews says this:

To view the video for this chapter GO TO **SIMPLYBELIEF.COM/ER12** Or scan the QR code with phone camera.

And without faith it is impossible to please God, because anyone who comes to him must believe that he exists and that he rewards those who earnestly seek him.[1]

The word "come" in the sentence above is the same Greek word that often gets translated "draw near." In this context, the author is not talking about becoming a believer or gaining eternal life. We know that because these words are spoken to believers. In addition, this chapter is focusing on a list of superstars of the faith who were certainly saved.

The author is encouraging saved people to endure difficult trials and to seek after God in spite of trouble. The verse shows that there is a reward for that kind of behavior. It tells us that if you don't believe that God rewards those who earnestly seek him, you will not be able to please Him or draw near to him. If you want a better relationship with God, the first step is to believe that He rewards. Remember reward is different from the free gift of salvation. Therefore, you must believe that He not only gives salvation, but He gives some bonus above and beyond eternal life to those who are diligent.

Let us explore this idea with an analogy. It could sound cold and mechanical, but I'm married not because I'm a selfless altruist. I'm married because I gain benefits from the arrangement. Being married has some really great perks. Companionship, intimacy, teamwork, emotional support, financial stability, and dozens of other benefits await those who enter into and maintain a healthy marriage. The fact is, I wouldn't be married if I didn't get something valuable from it. I wouldn't have gotten married if I didn't believe it was rewarding. Many who find it difficult to stay married would admit they have come to believe their marriage is no longer

---

1. Hebrews 11:6

rewarding.

The more I believe that my marriage has great rewards to offer, the more I will work on improving the relationship. I will seek intimacy and fellowship with my wife as long as I believe I have some reward to gain from it. If I stop believing I can get something from the relationship, I'm more likely to seek rewards outside the marriage. This single idea will diminish my relationship as much as any could. So why is it easy for me to stay committed to my wife? It's because I believe that we will be rewarded with greater companionship, intimacy, and emotional support if we diligently pursue an ever-better relationship with each other. I believe I will be rewarded for diligently drawing near to her. Similarly, I need to believe that God has something to offer me that is worth the work.

There are Bible teachers out there who would try to beat you up because you struggle to find the motivation to pursue God. Some pastors make you feel guilty for wanting some return on your investment. Some church librarians gripe at you for not working on your spiritual life for free.

As I read the Bible, what I see time and time again, is the mention of payoff. You're not expected to work for years with no paycheck. You aren't expected to compete when there is no prize. You're not asked to invest when there is no promise of return. Fortunately, you're not expected to diligently seek God without an eternal reward.

Notice what the verse says about what pleases God. "Without faith it is impossible to please God, because anyone who comes to Him must believe… He rewards those who earnestly seek him."[1] It would please God for you to draw near to Him. The only way you can draw near to Him is if you believe that there is a reward for doing so. He wouldn't expect you to believe it if it weren't true. So that means it

---

1. Hebrews 11:6

pleases God to reward you. Did you catch that? It pleases God to reward you. If you want to please God, do the things required so that He can give you a reward. Apparently, that makes Him very happy.

Once again you probably see the irony. People who say that they don't need a reward, but just want to please God are creating a logical impossibility. The way for them to please God is by believing and gaining rewards.

So, if you want to grow as you draw near to God, it's imperative that you believe that God has more for you. He has something more than just salvation. As amazing a gift as your salvation is, the reward you earn hereafter will only increase the value of your eternal experience. For those who claim they obey God simply to please Him, there is this simple reminder. You can't please Him unless you believe in rewards.

Each citizen of Heaven can either

EARN ETERNAL REWARDS IN HEAVEN

By obeying Christ on earth.

1 Corinthians 3:13-14

OR

MISS OUT ON ETERNAL REWARDS IN HEAVEN

By disobeying Christ on earth.

1 Corinthians 3:15

MINA

CHAPTER 13

Jesus shared a parable that will help us understand something important about rewards.

He said: "A certain nobleman went into a far country to receive for himself a kingdom and to return. So

---

To view the video for this chapter
GO TO **SIMPLYBELIEF.COM/ER13**
Or scan the QR code with phone camera.

he called ten of his servants, delivered to them ten minas, and said to them, 'Do business till I come.'[1]

There are a few things to notice here. The ten represent the total number of believers whom He calls servants.[2] From the time the world began until the moment Jesus returns to inaugurate His kingdom there will be a host of people who have and will receive everlasting life by faith. These ten servants represent all believers throughout history.

The second thing to notice is that the nobleman gives a command and equal resources to carry out that command. He says, "Do business till I come." They are to work continually until the nobleman returns. So if someone works only a short time or not at all, they would be displaying clear disobedience. This order is given to all ten servants without any caveats. No one gets more money than any other, and no one gets more expectations placed upon them than the others. They all get one mina-not a fortune but a reasonable sum of money, and they all get the same instructions. The playing field is completely fair and equal.

Jesus, in a similar manner, has placed an equal command upon all those who have believed in Him for everlasting life. Each saved person has an equal opportunity to work for Christ in his specific field of influence. Since it's an even playing field, how a person responds is entirely up to them. As the story develops we meet more players in the cast. Jesus says:

---

1. Luke 19:12-13

2. Alberto S. Valdés, "The Gospel according to Luke," in *The Grace New Testament Commentary*, ed. Robert N. Wilkin (Denton, TX: Grace Evangelical Society, 2010), 323.

"But his citizens hated him, and sent a delegation after him, saying, 'We will not have this man to reign over us.'[1]

Jesus would soon be rejected by the majority of Jews in Jerusalem, but the Jews of Jerusalem were not the last to reject Jesus as Christ or Messiah. In fact, today much of the world still rejects Jesus. Unbelievers throughout the globe who would likely answer the coming of Jesus in the same way, "We will not have this man reign over us!" In fact, John tells us when Jesus returns to rule the earth, the armies of the world will be arrayed against him.[2] Lining up tanks is a pretty clear message; they don't want to be ruled by him. These rebellious subjects are those who reject Christ. Jesus goes on:

"And so it was that when he returned, having received the kingdom, he then commanded these servants, to whom he had given the money, to be called to him, that he might know how much every man had gained by trading.[3]

You would think that the first thing the newly appointed king would do is dispense with his enemies. Instead, he takes care of the affairs of his household before he turns his attention to domestic matters. He calls his servants in and has them give account. The parable continues:

Then came the first, saying, 'Master, your mina has earned ten minas.' And he said to him, 'Well done, good servant; because you were

---

1. Luke 19:14
2. Revelation 19:19
3. Luke 19:15

faithful in a very little, have authority over ten cities.'

Remember the king's command, "Do business till I come." Not only did this servant obey but he excelled. He was extremely profitable. The king calls him "good servant," and he is the only one to get this title in the parable.

It's important to notice what the reward for his faithfulness is. He's given public recognition by the king and a county to rule. He gets ten cities to reign over. The reward of his well-done work was more work to do.[1] The king rewards him with a really sweet job.

A mina wasn't a fortune but was enough to start a small business, so finding out that a servant who had only managed a small account would become royalty is surprising. We should not miss the lesson, though. Jesus explains the principle as, "You were faithful in a very little, have authority over ten cities." It's almost humorous in its abruptness.

It's like saying, "You made a few thousand bucks mowing lawns over the summer, which qualifies you to be the governor of Texas." Though it may seem like quite a leap, the truth is even more sublime. Jesus is teaching His listeners that there is a great reward for those who excel at the basics. All of this is to say, do well in small things, and you will be rewarded with big things when the king comes.

Let's see how the next servant does.

---

1. William Barclay, *The Gospel of Luke*, The New Daily Study Bible (Louisville, KY; London: Westminster John Knox Press, 2001), 282.

And the second came, saying, 'Master, your mina has earned five minas.' Likewise he said to him, 'You also be over five cities.'[1]

Remember that each servant started with an equal amount of money and opportunity. So the fact that this servant produced less profit with his time and effort is entirely the fault of the servant. Nonetheless, he still did reasonably well.

Notice that there is something missing from this exchange. The king did not call this servant "good" as he did with the first servant. That's why I like to call him the "reliable servant." He did an adequate enough job. Clearly, he could have done better, but he could have done worse as well. Figuratively, he is your average B student. He works hard enough, but from time to time you might find him cooling his heels.

His reward is smaller than the first servant's. His rulership, although sizable is half that of the previous appointment. Once again we see the same principle at play. Being faithful in whatever we are given to do will result in reward that exists at an order of magnitude greater than what we did to earn it. However, the quality and quantity of our work directly affect the amount of responsibility and reward we are given when Jesus returns. Jesus goes on. This is where it begins to hurt:

"Then another came, saying, 'Master, here is your mina, which I have kept put away in a handkerchief. For I feared you, because you are a harsh man. You collect what you did not deposit, and reap what you did not sow.'[2]

First and foremost, this servant did not obey. Remember, the King told his servants to "Do business till I come." This

1. Luke 19:18-19
2. Luke 19:20-21

servant did not do business at all. Instead, he hid the money in a handkerchief. "Handkerchief" is a generous translation. The word means a cloth used to wipe sweat from the face.[1] He intentionally chose not to work for his master. He deliberately defied his king's command. Why didn't he obey the instructions to "Do business till I come?"

The way he viewed the king blocked him from doing any business with the money. The servant continued by saying, "For I feared you, because you are a harsh man. You collect what you did not deposit, and reap what you did not sow."

Basically, he said that he didn't see the point. He thought the king would not allow him to benefit from his own work. All effort, from the servant's perspective, would be a waste since it would just go to benefit the king alone. Why would he work if the king was just going to steal the profits and throw them in the royal treasury? He believed the king, in his shrewdness, would take away whatever he earned. Thus this servant decided not to do business at all.

The third servant didn't work because he didn't believe in rewards. He was not motivated enough to get busy. His lack of belief in a king who would reward him sabotaged his ability to do anything valuable. Laziness appeared to him to be the most rewarding course of action.

This seems to be the place that many Christians find themselves today. Many are stuck between a rock and a hard place. They fear God enough not to abandon the title "Christian," but they don't believe in rewards and therefore don't do many or any good works. What one believes about rewards is very important in terms of motivating the believer to work.

It's important to remember that this servant was simply

---

1. James Strong, *A Concise Dictionary of the Words in the Greek Testament and The Hebrew Bible* (Bellingham, WA: Logos Bible Software, 2009), 66.

wrong. Clearly, everything including the servants themselves is owned by the king. However, at the first two appointments, the king did not take away the profits from his servants. Instead, he allowed them to keep the profits. At the end of the parable, the first servant is identified as "the one who *has* ten minas."[1] Also, Jesus says, "To everyone who has [more] will be given."[2] The faithful servants were allowed to keep the profits and still have them at the end of Jesus' parable. They would use the profits to continue the work the king had just given them.

The third servant was just flat wrong to believe that the king would not reward his work. Although, by being lazy, he ensured he would get no reward from the king. He becomes a self-fulfilling prophecy in a way. Jesus continues with the parable:

> And he said to him, 'Out of your own mouth I will judge you, you wicked servant. You knew that I was a harsh man, collecting what I did not deposit and reaping what I did not sow. Why then did you not put my money in the bank, that at my coming I might have collected it with interest?'[3]

Notice that the king calls the one who's been unfaithful to him, "wicked servant." The king can legitimately call him "wicked" since the servant deliberately disobeyed his instructions. The king had commanded all of his servants, "Do business till I come." The king had not explained how profitable each servant had to be, only that they work continuously. This servant could have satisfied his master's instructions with minimum effort. He could have put the

---

1. Luke 19:24

2. Luke 19:26

3. Luke 19:22-23

money in the bank and allowed it to accrue interest. He would not have been rewarded as much as the first or second servant, but he would have gotten some reward. However, even that was too much work for this lazy, disobedient servant. So, with all of this in mind, the king calls him a "wicked servant."

Although the servant has disobeyed and will have to suffer the consequences, apparently the consequences are not being cast out of the royal household. Although his reputation is singed and his pride destroyed, the wicked one remains a *servant*. He remains part of the house of the king. We know this because the king still calls him a *servant*, albeit a wicked one. Even in the next section when the king delivers his sentence to his enemies, the servant remains a servant.

It's easy to become concerned that disobedience could lead to a loss of salvation. However, losing salvation is not in view in this parable. Instead, a potential loss of reward is prominently on display. Jesus continues:

> "And he said to those who stood by, 'Take the mina from him, and give *it* to him who has ten minas.' (But they said to him, 'Master, he has ten minas.') 'For I say to you, that to everyone who has will be given; and from him who does not have, even what he has will be taken away from him.[1]

Finally, we come to the conclusion of the wicked servant's story. His rebellion against his king has cost him even what he had. The mina, which he didn't make any use of, is taken away and given to the good servant. The king is interested in results. He apparently doesn't like to waste resources on servants who disobey.

---

1. Luke 19:24-26

Jesus gives the lesson through the words of the king. He says, "To everyone who has will be given; and from him who does not have, even what he has will be taken away from him."[1] It seems that He's acknowledging that this will seem harsh to some. The accusation made against the king has a kernel of truth from this perspective. While salvation is a free gift, reward has to be earned. Reward is given out based on merit. The wicked servant didn't earn any reward. Believers who are completely disobedient during their mortal life will not earn reward in the kingdom.

Now that the king has returned, this servant would long to be part of the happy affairs of the royal court, yet he's left on the outside. He's still a servant, and part of the kingdom, but he's woefully stripped of his royal duties. The wicked servant is not given a governorship of ten or five cities. No doubt he would love to receive a single city or possibly a neighborhood to manage. He's not even given a bathroom floor to mop.

We see his loss, and if we are not careful, it could be our own when we stand before Christ. The New Testament is loaded with references to the believer's opportunity to reign with Christ.[2] That's why it's safe to take this part of the parable quite literally. There will be those good servants who will be appointed to a high office in the Kingdom of God. There will be those who were reliable enough to work as middle managers in Christ's administration. Still, others will have proved their faithfulness so lacking that they are given no honorable task when Christ returns.

Jesus continues with this gruesome ending:

---

1. Luke 19:24-26

2. 2 Timothy 2:12, Revelation 20:4-6

Bring here those enemies of mine, who did not want me to reign over them, and slay *them* before me.""[1]

The wicked servant survives while the enemies of the king get slaughtered. It seems that Jesus is reminding us of the absolute nature of servanthood. The enemies, which represent unbelievers, are the only ones in danger of slaughter while all of the servants, regardless of their performance, remain alive. Though the wicked servant has acted pitifully, he survives and witnesses the destruction of those who rejected the rule. Even the "wicked servant" was saved.

If you've believed in Jesus for everlasting life, you are eternally secure. No matter how you live as a servant of the coming king, your eternal destiny is guaranteed. This parable reminds us it's your reward in the kingdom which is at stake, not your salvation. Your salvation is gained by faith alone in Christ alone, while your reward is earned by the hard work of obedience to Christ.

Let's summarize the four groups we met in this parable.

Good Servant = Saved and greatly rewarded
Reliable Servant = Saved and rewarded
Wicked Servant = Saved only
Enemies = Not saved

We can distill the lesson down to a pretty simple point. The lesson for believers is this: It will pay to obey. If you are a believer, then you stand to gain great reward if you are obedient to Christ. If you are a believer and you are neglecting His instructions, then you may be setting yourself up for a huge loss when Jesus arrives to establish His kingdom. If you have believed in Jesus for everlasting life, but failure

1. Luke 19:11-27

has marked your discipleship efforts ever since, take heart. Your salvation is not in jeopardy. However, it's time you get extra serious about your discipleship because you don't want to experience what other wicked servants will. You don't want to be a wicked servant. You want to be a good servant.

I'll leave you with this little piece of poetry.

For those who've believed
salvation is received,
but if obedience is ignored
there will be no reward.

RULING IS
NO FUN

CHAPTER 14

A while back I was speaking at a church out of state. After a talk about the parable of the mina, which was covered in the previous chapter, I received this email from someone who attended.

> I really enjoyed your message about the parable of the minas! But I didn't get to ask the question that was on my mind - what if one doesn't want the responsibility of "ruling over cities"? (Responsibilities make me feel anxious!)

The parable of the minas (which was discussed in a previous section) ends with faithful servants being given the opportunity to rule cities. Likewise, the unfaithful servant is

---

To view the video for this chapter
GO TO **SIMPLYBELIEF.COM/ER14**
Or scan the QR code with phone camera.

not allowed the right to rule any cities. This is a reference to the way in which faithful believers will be given the opportunity to rule with Christ in the Kingdom of Heaven. Paul put it this way:

If we endure, we will also reign with him.[1]

Though this sounds exciting and offers a powerful incentive for obedience, it doesn't motivate everyone. This woman's question about not wanting to rule is a great one, and she is not the first to ask it. In fact, it's very common for individuals to have no desire to rule and reign. If you're like me, you have no political aspirations. I've never run for office and never plan to. It would be too much trouble to run a city, state, or country. The idea makes my stomach churn.

Do you feel like this woman does? Do you struggle to feel motivated by a promise of ruling with Christ? What if one doesn't want the responsibility of ruling over cities or nations? How can we overcome this disinterest?

It's important to think of Jesus' future government on Earth as a practical and physical one. Maybe comparing His rule to a modern political administration might help. When we elect a president, he has about 4000 positions in His administration that need to be filled. Many of them are appointed by Him and His team. Each person is appointed to a different task that fits their abilities. He has everything from interns who run errands to a cabinet of close advisors. Although every one whom the president appoints is doing a different job, it could be said that they all govern, some more directly than others.

The Vise President has a very different role from the press secretary. The defense minister has a different role from the

---

1. 2 Timothy 2:12

minister of education. Each of their roles fits their particular skills. In most cases the people appointed have been working all their lives to get where they are. They are not only equipped to do the job, but they find the work very rewarding. Each of these people is governing in a general sense, even though not all are governors.

I imagine Christ's administration in a similar way. Jesus will appoint people to positions that fit their particular skills and abilities. In the same way that an administration governs as a team with different people performing different tasks, I think Jesus' appointees will fulfill different tasks which all fall under the definition of "reign." There is not much information given about the particular roles that Jesus will appoint in the Kingdom of Heaven. However, there is enough to make a rough sketch. Here are some of the kingdom positions of which we are aware:

King of kings (Jesus)[1]
Subordinate kings[2]
Judges and Counselors[3]
Royal Priests[4]
Officers and Magistrates[5]
Shepherds[6]

It's possible that some of the titles above overlap or even describe the same jobs, but there will certainly be many more

1. 1 Timothy 6:15

2. For Jesus to be King of Kings, there must be Kings that he is sovereign over.

3. Isaiah 1:26

4. 1 Peter 2:9, Revelation 5:10

5. Isaiah 60:17

6. Jeremiah 3:15

than those listed. The important thing to see is that all of these jobs qualify as "reigning with Christ" even though they are not all kings. A shepherd might serve and lead a small group of people by teaching them wisdom while a king might serve a large group of people by making wise administrative decisions. Every job that Jesus will appoint His servants to will be one in which the appointee serves others. Leadership in the kingdom of God is not like dictatorship here and now. It's about serving others and serving Christ. Think about how Jesus said:

> The kings of the Gentiles exercise lordship over them… But not so among you; on the contrary, he who is greatest among you, let him be as the younger, and he who governs as he who serves.[1]

Being a governor in the kingdom of Heaven is not about the benefits that come with being a lord or lady. Instead, it's about service. The one on whom is bestowed heavenly royalty is the one who has a more extensive opportunity to serve God and others. This is the essence of reigning with Christ.

Most people who say they are not interested in ruling say that because they would rather spend their time helping and edifying other people. They don't want to rule because they would rather serve others instead. Here's the beauty of Jesus' kingdom. Serving, edifying, teaching, sharing wisdom, guiding, shepherding, and counseling are all included in reigning with Christ. The job He gives you in His administration will be awesome. He'll see to it that the role you play is a perfect fit for the desires of your heart. We will explore more reasons why reigning with Christ will, amazing in the upcoming section about heavenly Royalty.

---

1. Luke 22:25-26

IN **HEAVEN**

Less Reward

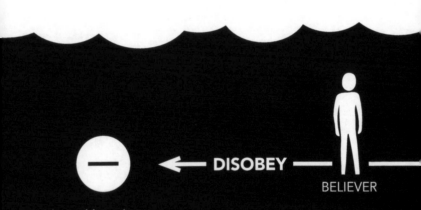

DISOBEY

BELIEVER

Less Happiness

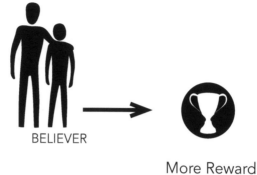

BELIEVER

More Reward

OBEY CHRIST ➔ ➕

More Happiness

ON **EARTH**

OVERCOMER
CHAPTER 15

There were two brothers from a small town in Oklahoma whom I used to know. They were brilliant, both top notch academics even at a young age. They both applied for college early and pursued blossoming careers. Each of them received complete scholarships to attend any university of their choice. One of the brothers followed his interests into aerospace engineering. After finishing that program, he continued on toward a doctorate degree. Brilliant as he was, it was still incredibly difficult. He pressed on toward the goal. After achieving an impressive array of degrees, he has had a range of interesting jobs. The last I heard, he is teaching at a large university. He exemplifies the word *success*. No matter the academic challenge placed before him, he overcame it with sheer determination.

The second brother had a very different story altogether. He too was a genius. I don't use that word poetically; I

To view the video for this chapter
GO TO **SIMPLYBELIEF.COM/ER15**
Or scan the QR code with phone camera.

mean literally. He operated at genius level, which is usually considered somewhere above 140 IQ. This brother also had a full-ride scholarship and had a strong start in his studies. Research programs at various universities pursued him. He produced some impressive work in the first couple of years of his studies, but somewhere along the way, he ran into some personal problems. Even though he had a full ride scholarship, the emotional intensity of academia was piling up. His difficulties caught up to him, the pressure grew too much, and he was not able to finish his degree. Now he's back in the same small Oklahoma town where he grew up. His life is probably pleasant enough, but he is not enjoying the same quality of success as his brother. Though both brothers had a scholarship, one fought and overcame, while the other was overcome. In this chapter, we will look at what it means to be an overcomer.

The apostles, especially John, often used the term, "overcome." In his writings, John quotes Jesus as saying things like, "to the one who overcomes I will give...", "To him who overcomes I will grant to him...," and "He who overcomes shall inherit...." In fact, John uses the term almost 20 times. The rewards for being an overcomer are astounding. However, before we find out what an overcomer will get, we need to discover what an overcomer is. So, what does it mean to overcome?

Synonyms for "overcome" include victory, triumph, prevail, conquer, succeed, win, and others. One who overcomes could be described as a winner, champion, conquerer, victor, medalist, and many other positive things. The word overcome is derived from a Greek word that almost everyone in the world would recognize. Have you heard of the sports brand Nike? Nike (νίκη) means victory[1] and is the same root word

1. Swanson, *Dictionary of Biblical Languages with Semantic.*

from which overcome is derived. Nike was also the name for the Greek god of victory.

In a nutshell, victory is what it means to overcome. That's why I like to think of the ones who overcome as the Christian winners. For many, it's hard to imagine that the heavenly system might be set up so that there are Christian winners and losers. Maybe this is new to you but don't fret if this feels a little surprising. We will flesh it out as we go. Let's start with this simple question, "What makes someone an overcomer?"

There is a minimum requirement that all contestants must meet before the competition really begins. Like preliminary screenings for Olympic athletes, a foundation must first be laid. John gives us that minimum requirement:

> Who is it that overcomes the world? Only the one
> who believes that Jesus is the Son of God.[1]

The first requirement is that someone is a believer. No one who is unsaved could be called an overcomer either in the salvation or discipleship sense. All believers experience victory over death. Due to the work of Christ, the believer will live forever.[2] So every believer has experienced an initial victory.

Though all believers have overcome death at their new birth, each has an opportunity to also overcome in the way they live. Each believer is made capable to conquer but not guaranteed victory in Christian living. It hardly needs to be said that this initial victory does not *guarantee* subsequent victory in Christian living.[3] Although the original victory of salvation is a substantial win gained for the believer, there is

---

1. 1 John 5:5 NIV

2. John 11:25-26

3. Zane Clark Hodges, *The Epistle of John: Walking in the Light of God's Love* (Irving, TX: Grace Evangelical Society, 1999), 216.

an expectation that the victory spread to the active parts of a believers life. Paul added to this idea when he wrote simply:

> Do not be overcome by evil, but overcome evil with good.[1]

These words remind me of my brother-in-law. He became a believer when he was eleven years old. He was wealthy, had a beautiful wife, and a lovely 8-month-old daughter. Somewhere along the way, he began to give up on living as God instructs. It was in little things at first. He would drink a bit too much. He would be mean to his wife. He would go absent for days. As the pressures of life swelled, he allowed depression and evil thoughts to win the victory over his mind. On Easter day he put a gun to his head and allowed himself to be overcome by evil. He ended his life with an act of self-murder. He could have kept fighting, but he refused. My brother-in-law was with the Lord the moment he pulled that trigger, but I guarantee there is regret and loss of potential reward for what he did. He did not overcome evil with good but instead allowed himself to be overcome by evil.

That is an extreme example. Thank God that not everyone's experience will end in suicide. However, many believers experience what Paul calls being "overcome by evil." All overcomers are believers, but now we will see that not all believers will be overcomers. Our faith in Christ has opened the door by bringing the victory of salvation. However, that does not guarantee victory in our daily life. Paul instructs that believers should fight to overcome daily. Faith in Christ has given us eternal salvation. Everyone who is saved has the chance to overcome. However, there are believers who will be overcome by evil. That's why we say, all overcomers are

---

1. Romans 12:21

believers, but not all believers will be overcomers.

How do we conquer evil? We don't fight fire with fire, and we don't fight evil with evil. We fight evil with good. Responding to evil acts with good works is an obvious mark of an overcomer. The successful disciple will show this kind of self-control in a range of situations from being annoyed to being persecuted. There is never a shortage of opportunities to demonstrate your Christian will to overcome.

Paul offers not three but two options. Either a believer will be overcome by evil, or will overcome evil with good. There is no middle ground. There are no neutral Christians. You can't be Switzerland. There is no fence on which to sit. Sin will have the victory over us, or we will have the victory over sin. We will either be one of the overcomers, or we will be one of the overcome.

Is there an example of an overcomer from which we may draw inspiration? There sure is. Jesus defined himself as an overcomer when He said:

"In the world you will have tribulation; but be of good cheer, I have overcome the world."[1]

Do you remember the WWJD bracelets? For those of you who don't remember the craze, WWJD stands for "What Would Jesus Do?" Although it's a bit cliche, it's a pretty good question. Some form of this is a great way to keep on track as an overcomer. Ask yourself what Jesus would do in the situation you are in currently. If you don't know, then seek an answer in scripture. Imitating His actions is one of the best ways to ensure you are on the path of successful discipleship. Knowing what Jesus did and following that example is what an overcomer does.

1. John 16:33

Paul carries this idea to the next level with his words to the Roman church. He gives this moving charge toward the middle of his letter. He says:

> For your sake we are killed all day long; We are accounted as sheep for the slaughter. Yet, in all these things we are more than conquerors through Him who loved us.[1]

Paul gives us this powerful example of what it means to be an overcomer. When he says "more than conquerors" he uses a hybrid idea that slams two similarly strong words together. The meaning here could be rendered "prevail completely."[2] We not only experience the victory won for us at the moment of our salvation but we are capable of prevailing even in the midst of incredible suffering. It's not a half victory or even an early victory that is taken over by a later defeat. It's a complete victory in both salvation and discipleship. He specifies that we are able to completely overcome things like being persecuted and killed. He doesn't mean that we should run away to escape our own death. Instead, if God calls us to be martyrs, we have the power needed to face it with triumph.

Do all Christians face martyrdom with honor and poise? No, many have shrunk from it. Do all believers behave admirably in the midst of persecution? Obviously not. Do all believers prevail in suffering? Nope. However, Paul reminds us that we are capable of conquering in all of these. How? We conquer by the things mentioned above, but also by remembering the indelible promise of Christ. Paul follows this declaration of victory by an expression of his eternal security.

---

1. Romans 8:36-37

2. Zane C. Hodges, *Romans: Deliverance from Wrath*, ed. Robert N. Wilkin (Corinth, TX: Grace Evangelical Society, 2013), 248.

It was his assurance of salvation that gave him the foundation for conquering all things. Notice what he said directly after the previous verse:

> For I am persuaded that neither death nor life, nor angels nor principalities nor powers, nor things present nor things to come, nor height nor depth, nor any other created thing, shall be able to separate us from the love of God which is in Christ Jesus our Lord.[1]

This is what allowed Paul to be confident that he could overcome. If you have believed in Jesus, no matter what, you will always live in the love of Jesus Christ. Knowing this impossibly empowering truth, we are given the strength to be more than conquerors. Whether you use that strength is up to you. Whether you live in victory or in defeat is entirely your choice.

To sum up, an overcomer is one who is not only saved but lives out their faith boldly. They talk about their Lord even when it could cost them their job, their reputation, and their lives. The overcomer is a successful disciple who not only has free eternal life but also fights to be obedient for the remainder of their mortal life. An overcomer is one who abides in God's word and fights the temptations of the wicked one. An overcomer is one who triumphs over evil acts with good deeds.

---

1. Romans 8:38-39

WHEN IT HURTS

CHAPTER 16

At the end of a speaking engagement, I had a man strike up a conversation. He mentioned that his wife is confined to her bed with terrible health problems. She is a believer, but she suffers continuously. Her husband is her full-time care-giver, and he helps her with everything from getting dressed to performing her bodily functions. She is miserable. Her life has been horrid for over a decade now. Her husband, the man I was talking with, said, "She is in such suffering, and she feels like there is nothing she can do to serve God. What

---

To view the video for this chapter
GO TO **SIMPLYBELIEF.COM/ER16**
Or scan the QR code with phone camera.

can she do?" I responded that she could spend her days in prayer. There is a high reward which waits for those who pray in private.[1]

I'm sure my answer felt a little unsatisfying. The woman, no doubt, wants to leave her bed. She would be thrilled to share the gospel with strangers, visit widows and orphans, or even vacuum the church building. Instead, she's stuck in her bed with nothing she can do but pray and listen to an audiobook version of the Bible. Even in all of this suffering, she has stayed committed to her faith. Virtually all of the present rewards for Christian living are not available to her. Her physical quality of life is awful, she is mentally frustrated, and she is socially isolated. How disappointing it would be if there were no special reward for someone like her; someone who diligently endures suffering while remaining committed to the Lord.

Will it be worth it? It doesn't seem fair that a believer who suffers horrid things but stays faithful should receive the same outcome as a believer who has a comfortable life but lives a lukewarm faith. Shouldn't the ones who faithfully endure suffering receive something for their trouble? Jesus and his apostles certainly said so. Paul talks about suffering like this:

> We are hard-pressed on every side... we are perplexed... persecuted... struck down... always carrying about in the body the dying of the Lord Jesus... For we who live are always delivered to death for Jesus' sake...[2]

This is the kind of suffering that Paul experienced. He met resistance everywhere he went. He was beaten with 39

---

1. Matthew 6:6

2. 2 Corinthians 4:8-12

lashes of a leather whip five different times. He was beaten nearly to death with long wooden rods on three different occasions. He was stoned until the people throwing rocks at his head determined he was dead, but he lived through it. He was involved in three different shipwrecks, where he was stranded at sea in open waters for a night and a day. His own people rejected him. He had health issues that debilitated him, and he was probably almost completely blind. He was put in jail for his faith. He endured hunger, cold, and nakedness in prison and out. Finally, he was murdered for his faith in Christ. Concerning all of the suffering that he had endured, Paul says:

> For our light affliction, which is but for a moment,
> is working for us a far more exceeding and eternal
> weight of glory.[1]

Paul's problems, like those of many, do not sound like a "light affliction." His suffering was intense and overwhelming. In spite of that, he calls that suffering, *light affliction*. How could he consider such things to be *light affliction?* It's because his ever-present focus was on what was coming. He knew that his suffering, if he endured it in faith, would produce an incredible outcome. The reward he would receive would make it all worth while.

The trouble that you face may be crushing you. Your knees may be buckling under the weight of your devastating problem. Maybe you've buried your family in debt. Maybe you've lost loved ones. Maybe you suffer from the depression of loneliness. Whatever your suffering is, it is a light affliction compared to what's in store for those who endure the pain in faith. If you can stand up under the paralyzing pain of

---

1. 2 Corinthians 4:17

suffering, you will be rewarded with something that far outweighs the pain you endured. If you can remain anchored to Christ through the storm, you will find that in the end, it was all worth it. The suffering, the pain, the agony of life will blossom into a far more exceeding and eternal weight of glory.

Paul expands on this idea in another letter. He points out the contrast between his present suffering and the future reward with the concept of being co-heirs with Christ. Notice the contrast that he offers between present suffering and future reward.

> Now if we are children, then we are heirs—heirs of God and co-heirs with Christ, if indeed we share in his sufferings in order that we may also share in his glory. I consider that our present sufferings are not worth comparing with the glory that will be revealed in us.[1]

Follow the train of thought here. He says that if we suffer with Christ, which is no easy task, we will get to share in His inheritance and even have a share in His glory in Heaven. What a reward! Notice that this is not a reward He will give to everyone, only those who suffer with Him. Those who face suffering and endure in the faith will be rewarded. Those who manage not to be scattered by the desiccating wind of life's pain but stand up to the world of agony will receive incomparable glory. This is especially true if the suffering we endure is on account of Christ.

He says that the present suffering, as bad as it may be, is not worth comparing with the glory that will be revealed in us. No matter how bad it is; no matter how hard you try; no matter how much you have to fight, sweat, toil, and suffer the

---

1. Romans 8:17-18

payoff will be so great that you can't even compare it to what you had to do to get it.

Imagine getting a world-class sports car for one dollar. The price you paid is not worthy to be compared with the worth of that glorious car. Imagine paying a buck for a lottery ticket and winning a cool million. The price you paid is not worthy to be compared with what you won. Imagine setting up a savings account with only a dollar, only to find that the interest rate is so good your dollar has become a billion. Imagine suffering for 85 years in your mortal body, only to find out that you will be rewarded eternally for your faithfulness in pain. An eternal reward is an infinite reward. Thus the suffering you are going through right now is not worthy to be compared with the glory that you will share with Christ, as long as you stay faithful.

James wrote on the subject in his letter:

> Consider it pure joy, my brothers, and sisters, whenever you face trials of many kinds because you know that the testing of your faith produces perseverance. Let perseverance finish its work so that you may be mature and complete, not lacking anything.[1]

Everyone who goes through *trials* suffers. It's difficult to imagine how James expects each of us to be joyful in the face of suffering trials. He says that those who endure this kind of suffering will gain perseverance and thus grow to mature completeness. Then he gives the key to the entire concept. The one who endures suffering with joy will lack nothing. The inverse must be true as well. The believer who faces trials but meets them with bitterness will lack something. This is the motivation for enduring suffering in faith. But, what does he

---

1. James 1:2-4

mean by saying we will *lack nothing?* Like Paul, James gives us the answer only a few verses later.

> Blessed is the one who perseveres under trial because, having stood the test, that person will receive the crown of life that the Lord has promised to those who love him.[1]

James was motivated by the reward that faithful endurance would render. He did not expect us to endure suffering simply because we are altruistic. Instead, he encourages us to look to the reward and to be motivated by it. If we keep the reward in mind, we will be more likely to endure suffering and to do so in the faith. It may sound callous or cavalier, but no matter what your suffering is, it is not worthy to be compared to the reward you will receive for being faithful in the midst of that suffering. If you can keep perspective and meet that suffering head-on with joy, you will lack nothing.

You may have considered giving up. You may have considered walking away from God. You may have considered suicide. Please, remember that the suffering is temporary and you will be reimbursed for your trouble and pain. In human courts, a lawyer can file a civil suit to sue for pain and suffering. God's court is the place of supreme justice, and He pays back lavishly for pain and suffering, as long as that suffering is endured in faith. So, stand strong, brother or sister. It's going to be worth it.

---

1. James 1:12

MOUNTAIN SIDE CHAT

CHAPTER 17

If I asked twenty people, "What is the sermon on the mount about?" I would probably get twenty different answers. When teaching about the sermon on the mount, most Bible teachers focus on the various subsections of the sermon but miss the single consistent theme in the whole lesson. It's for that reason that I can say with some confidence that the sermon on the mount is probably not about what you think it's about. If you're an avid Bible student, I bet you could drum up a handful of quotes from Jesus' famous sermon, but very few people can name the consistent thread that runs through the sermon. If you can, I'd be impressed.

One of the marks of the sermon on the mount is that it has a bunch of hard teachings. Many of the things that

To view the video for this chapter
GO TO **SIMPLYBELIEF.COM/ER17**
Or scan the QR code with phone camera.

Jesus tells His listeners to do are so incredibly difficult; that it's unlikely anyone can claim they have obeyed His sermon. His mountainside lessons can leave a person feeling that they don't measure up to these insurmountable instructions.

The nearly impossible standard that Jesus gives for godly living doesn't sound like much fun. In fact, it sometimes isn't. A person can spend an entire life trying to live up to the instructions found in Jesus' sermon, but it isn't easy. If a person commits to living like Jesus teaches, he or she will miss out on a lot of leisure, pleasure, and enjoyment.

Since the sermon on the mount is full of painful instructions, there better be some good motivation to follow them. There are some present rewards for godly living, but those here-and-now incentives begin to look a little thin when we consider what Jesus is telling us to do. If there's no eternal payoff, no one would want even to attempt to live up to the standard Jesus presents.

Some trip because they mistakenly think the sermon on the mount offers instructions for salvation. There are those who claim that a person must obey Jesus' instructions or he is not saved. However, this presents a tremendous problem. Hypothetically speaking, how much of the sermon must be obeyed for a person to be saved? Would 80% do it? What about 70%? What percentage of the Sermon do you obey daily? My guess is most devoted Christians fall far short of the standard presented. It's for that reason that I must remind you, the sermon on the mount is not an instruction manual for gaining salvation. It's an instruction manual for those who have already believed and received eternal life. You can wipe the sweat from your forehead. If you are saved by faith, for free, then why obey the sermon on the mount? There better be a fantastic motivation.

What is the consistent thread that runs through the sermon

on the mount? One of the best ways to discover the theme of a talk is to look for repetition. A simple word search will give a clue. It's packed with terms like *rewards in Heaven*, *treasure in Heaven*, *inherit*, and a host of others. By my count, at least thirty references to eternal rewards are included in the sermon on the mount. Thus, the sermon on the mount is an instructional guide for discipleship living which includes eternal motivation for doing so.

Now you should begin to see how the two ends meet. In Jesus' most famous sermon, which contains instructions for discipleship living, Jesus indicates that the motivation for that difficult lifestyle is eternal rewards. It's not only rewarding here on earth, but rewards in Heaven that should motivate our godly living. In fact, there will be times where there are no rewards on earth. It's those times when the reward in Heaven is going to get you through the throat punch that the Christian life sometimes gives.

Salvation comes as a free gift for those who believe in Jesus. Though if you are going to attempt the Everest climb that is the godly lifestyle, Jesus offers a powerful motivation. Here are a few examples of the motivation that Jesus offers in the sermon on the mount:

> Blessed are you when they revile and persecute you… Rejoice and be exceedingly glad, for great is your **reward** in Heaven….[1]

Notice that the motivation he offers for joyfully enduring persecution is reward in Heaven. Here is another phrase from the sermon on the mount:

---

1. Matthew 5:11-12

> ...Pray to your Father who is in secret. And your
> Father who sees in secret will **reward** you openly.[1]

It's difficult to pray. It's especially hard to pray regularly when no one is watching. The motivation that Jesus gives for this difficult task is reward. Let's look at one more example:

> Lay up for yourselves **treasures in Heaven**, where neither moth nor rust destroys and where thieves do not break in and steal.[2]

It's statements like these that run throughout the sermon. The consistent theme is clear. Look for the reward in everything you do. In every situation from what you eat to how you treat your brother, watch for chances to gain heavenly reward. This is not some invention of my own. Jesus uses this theme as the yellow brick road that runs through the Christian life. Every action done for Jesus in this life is a chance for reward in the next. If there were some better motivation for godly living, wouldn't Jesus have mentioned it? It's reward that He offers to those who obey.

He gives this instruction that sums up the sermon quite nicely.

> Seek first the Kingdom of God and His righteousness....[3]

Obviously, that won't be easy, but if we allow the reward, He offers to fuel our pursuit. Then it will certainly be worth the trouble. This is why looking to the reward is such a powerful motivation for godly living available.

---

1. Matthew 6:6

2. Matthew 6:20

3. Matthew 6:33

THE REWARD FOR VICTORY

CHAPTER 18

My daughter can be challenging to motivate, as is true of nearly any three year old. Quite often I offer her a reward for accomplishing a task. I've noticed that making a promise of general reward is not as effective as being specific about the payoff. If I say, "You will get a reward for cleaning up your room," she immediately has to know what the reward is. If I don't have some well-thought-out payoff, then she lags in her duties. However, saying, "If you clean your room, I'll give you a red sucker," usually produces diligent dutifulness.

It's human nature to question the reward to see if the work will be worth it. My daughter wants to know if the reward is something she actually wants. If it isn't, she will find it difficult

To view the video for this chapter
GO TO **SIMPLYBELIEF.COM/ER18**
Or scan the QR code with phone camera.

to be motivated to finish the task. For her, cookies, candies, and trips to the zoo seem to be the top octane fuel for getting work done.

It stands to reason that the same would be true for adults. If a businessperson offers you a job, what are the two things you want to know? What is the job and how much does it pay? You can quickly do the labor-to-pay formula in your head. If the job is digging trenches in the sun-dried red clay of East Texas for 12 hours a day and the pay is $3.50 an hour, you probably wouldn't take that job. However, if the job is petting kittens two hours a day and it pays $5000 an hour well you'd probably take it.

Did you know that Jesus said you'll be repaid for good work? That's right. He once said, "When you give a feast, invite the poor, the maimed, the lame, the blind. And you will be blessed because they cannot repay you; for you shall be repaid at the resurrection of the just."[1]

Did you catch that? He said, "You shall be repaid." It's as if he's keeping your receipts in a filing cabinet in Heaven. When you arrive, he'll pull your file and issue reimbursements. The repayment He gives outweighs the work we do. Doing what He says to do in this verse is hard. Nonetheless, Jesus said we'll be paid for hard work.

What will the rewards be? We've already alluded to the answer, but it's time that we spell it out. I'm convinced that these categories can describe the rewards in Heaven: Riches, Rights, Recognition, Regalia, Royalty, and Relationship. We can find each of these categories of eternal reward throughout scripture. Let's begin by taking a look at the first category, riches in Heaven.

---

1. Luke 14:13-15

THE REWARD OF **RICHES**

 THE REWARD OF **RIGHTS**

 THE REWARD OF **RECOGNITION**

 THE REWARD OF **REGALIA**

 THE REWARD OF **ROYALTY**

 THE REWARD OF **RELATIONSHIP**

Believers who are **OBEDIENT** on earth will be rewarded with

TRUE RICHES
IN THE KINGDOM OF HEAVEN.

MATTHEW 6:19-20, LUKE 12:33, 16:10-12

REWARD FOR VICTORY:
RICHES

CHAPTER 19

I was seventeen. It was summer. I needed a job, or so my parents told me. I was aiming for a part-time situation with little responsibility and minimal hours. After all, I was still a kid and wanted to enjoy as much of the summer as I could. I was hoping to still be able to sleep in, and not work afternoons.

Without much trouble, I got minimum wage work at a local veterinarian clinic scooping droppings out of animal cages. I accepted the job, figuring it would please my parents. Before I had even put in my first day at the clinic, I got a second offer from a regional environmental attorney. He would pay four bucks more an hour, I could set my own schedule, and best of all it was a media job. I would be tasked with making digital video packages for upcoming court cases. I'd get to use all kinds of high tech equipment, something I loved. Needless

To view the video for this chapter
GO TO **SIMPLYBELIEF.COM/ER19**
Or scan the QR code with phone camera.

to say, the media job made scooping animal poop seem like a crap job. However, since I had already accepted the job at the vet clinic, I decided to spend my summer doing both. I worked mornings in the poop factory and spent my afternoons in the air-conditioned studio making media magic.

This was my first time to have an income stream, not to mention two. I felt like I had true riches. It was interesting how rapidly money changed things in my life. I no longer needed to rely as much on my parent's help. I had an increase in self-confidence. I could do things in my leisure time that I had never been able to afford before. I was even able to take my high school girlfriend to the theater. Having to manage money was what began my shift from being a child to being a responsible adult.

As everyone is aware, having money has its problems both practical and spiritual. There are basically two main spiritual problems that arise from the possession of wealth. First, riches can make it hard for a person to get saved. Here's how Jesus put it:

> "...How hard it is for those who trust in riches to enter the kingdom of God![1]

It's struggle and suffering that often remind us that we need the Lord. A comfortable life, especially one padded by wealth, can numb our spiritual senses. Money softens the harsh blows of life, blows that some people need to become aware of their need for a savior. My mentor, a brilliant East Texas pastor, recently reminded me that believing in Jesus for salvation requires that we mentally admit that we need help, that we need salvation. Requesting help is easier for a broke, homeless, single mother than a billionaire tycoon. The habit

---

1. Mark 10:24

of asking for physical help sets trends that spill over into the spiritual life. This connects to how easy or difficult it is for someone to admit they need salvation.

Jesus warns of a second danger associated with riches. Here is a famous saying given to us by Christ:

> "No one can serve two masters; for either he will hate the one and love the other, or else he will be loyal to the one and despise the other. You cannot serve God and money.[1]

The second risk is that riches make it hard to serve God. Serving God is not what brings salvation, only faith in Christ can do that. However, serving God is what brings fulfillment in this life and reward in the next life. There's a kind of irony in this. For a believer, seeking only wealth in this life assures that he will have none in the next. Pursuing riches ensures heavenly poverty.

Building upon this idea, Jesus told a story of a rich man who came to trust in his own wealth. He spent his time thinking about how to get more wealth for himself; then unexpectedly the man died, and all of his belongings were given to someone else. Jesus then gives this lesson:

> "So is he who lays up treasure for himself, and is not rich toward God."[2]

Jesus warns that wanting wealth in this life can shipwreck our ability to have any in the next life. He instructs us to be wary of the dangers of earthly wealth. However, He adds a call to look toward the kind of riches that God gives. What kind of riches does God give? Will they be physical and

---

1. Matthew 6:24

2. Luke 12:21

tangible wealth in Heaven, or is this a metaphor for something as yet unknown. Basically, will there be money in Heaven?

It seems that most have the notion that everything will be free in Heaven. If everything is free, then there would be no need for money? But where did that idea come from? As I began to do research for this chapter, I offered google this question, "Will the Kingdom of Heaven have an economy?" After wading through about five thousand links to health and wealth preachers, I came across a great quote that stood out to me. Bruce Wilkinson seems to think the answer to that question is "yes." In September of 2002, he said in an interview,

> "There is an economy in Heaven. There are cities in Heaven, and there are people who lead and people who don't lead, people who are rewarded and people who are not rewarded."[1]

This quote brings up all sorts of exciting imagery that we could explore. However, the thing I want to focus on at this point is the question of money and whether it will be a facet of daily life in the Kingdom of Heaven.

When I was in my twenties, I worked as a videographer. I got hired to shoot a video teaching series by a group out of Dallas, TX, called Grace Evangelical Society. In that series Dr. Robert Wilkin, an Author and theologian said:

> "In my view, the word *treasure* refers to riches… Most likely it refers to money. I think in the Millennial and Eternal Kingdom believers are going to have some sort of monthly trust fund they live on, and that money will be used, of course, to glorify God. I know people don't tend to think of the Kingdom as having an economy. They don't think of spending money,

---

1. In an interview with Gordon Robertson of CBN. Link: goo.gl/JHNN4q

but why shouldn't we think that way? If Adam and Eve had not sinned wouldn't we have developed an economy on Earth? Wouldn't we have cities, roads and everything else? It seems to me there will be an economy in the Kingdom of Heaven."[1]

He acknowledged that his view is speculative since scripture doesn't explicitly speak to the subject, but he felt confident that this was the way things will be when Jesus returns to set up His Kingdom.

In my research for this book, I sent out scads of emails to my theologian friends and acquaintances trying to take their pulse on this concept. Most returned with confidence that there would be an economy in the kingdom when Jesus brings Heaven on Earth, but much of it was inference, and only a few biblical references surfaced. So it feels as if I am stepping into uncharted waters here, but that's exactly where the treasure is usually sunk. So let's sail on and see what we can find. The first port is Deuteronomy.

In Deuteronomy God is talking to the Nation of Israel about what they can expect if they obey. God makes this amazing statement to them as a promise for the future of their kingdom:

> For the Lord your God will bless you as he has promised, and you will lend to many nations but will borrow from none. You will rule over many nations but none will rule over you.[2]

Can you think of a time when Israel has ruled over many nations? I've searched the history books. It hasn't happened

---

1. Eternal Rewards In the Bible, By Grace Evangelical Society, Hosted by Youtube. Link: goo.gl/Gy6YrC

2. Deuteronomy 15:6

yet. This points us to the future. It hasn't happened yet, but God promised that it will. This must mean that this will happen in the coming Kingdom of God. Notice the first half of this promise where He says, "You will lend to many nations but will borrow from none." In telling Israel about their future reign in the Kingdom era, God revealed something that is significant.

For there to be lending and borrowing, there must be something to lend and borrow. Therefore there must be something beyond barter of commodities. There must be currency to be lent and borrowed. Where there is currency, there is economy. This is the first clue that there will be a money system replete with international banking in the Kingdom of Heaven.

Isaiah wrote:

> And you will be called priests of the Lord, you will
> be named ministers of our God. You will feed on the
> wealth of nations, and in their riches you will boast.[1]

I'll ask you again. Can you think of a time in history when Israel acted as priests for a worldwide religion and was fed on the wealth of the nations? Nope? I didn't think so. This also is something that hasn't happened yet. We know that this is talking about the future because of what Jesus said. It was from this same chapter that Jesus read in the synagogue at Nazareth. He read the first four verses and then declared that those four verses had been fulfilled. However, he didn't say that the following verses, which include the one above, had been fulfilled. That's because they wouldn't be fulfilled until the Kingdom had begun.

What does this verse mean when it says, "You will be called

---

1. Isaiah 61:6

priests… and will feed on the wealth of nations."? What's in view here is the tithe. In Old Testament Israel the tribe of Levi had a special job. They were the priests of God's temple. The Levites were allowed to collect a tenth of the other eleven tribe's income in return for their priestly services.[1] So the wealth of the nation went to feed the priests of God.

When Isaiah, talking to the entire nation of Israel says, "You will be called priests of the Lord… You will feed on the wealth of nations…," He's telling us that there will be a planet-wide tithe that nations will pay. In the Kingdom, the nations will send their tithes to support the work that Israel is doing. The nation of Israel, acting as ministers of God, will feed on the wealth sent in by the nations. In the eternal kingdom, there seems to be a reference to something similar when it says that the kings of the nations will bring their splendor into the new Jerusalem.[2] It's an amazing window into what the world will be like in the Kingdom of Heaven.

There must be some type of international exchange of currency on both the individual and governmental level. The economy of the Kingdom will likely be even more advanced than ours is today.

Evidence shows that there will be an international economy, but will individuals buy and sell? Though the Bible doesn't answer this question directly, it does indicate that the familiar functions of life will exist in the kingdom. There will be traveling, eating, and drinking in the Kingdom.[3] In addition to banking, there will be property ownership,[4] construction projects, farming, productive labor, and

---

1. Numbers 18:21

2. Revelation 21:24

3. Ibid.

4. John 14:1-3

childbearing.[1] In today's world, all of this costs money. In the world of tomorrow, it makes sense that much of this will still come at some expense.

However, we do discover that are certain commodities that will be able to be "bought" without cost. Jesus says that during the Eternal Kingdom access to the fountain of the water of life will be available to everyone for free.[2] Again in the next chapter, He repeats the idea when He says, "Whoever desires, let him take the water of life freely."[3] This may be related to Isaiah's words:

> "Ho! Everyone who thirsts, Come to the waters;
> And you who have no money, Come, buy and eat.
> Yes, come, buy wine and milk Without money and
> without price.[4]

This may be a reference to what will be available in the Kingdom to everyone without cost. This makes sense when we consider that the Earth will be so fruitful in the kingdom era that the basic needs of life will be met even for those who have no funds. Food crops will thrive with incredible quantity year round.[5] The deserts and wildernesses will become lush and productive land.[6] Even those who have no resources with which to buy are invited to partake in the abundance that the Earth offers in the Kingdom era.

The Kingdom economy will be quite different in some ways and very similar in others. It is in this economic system

---

1. Isaiah 65:21-22

2. Revelation 21:6

3. Revelation 22:17

4. Isaiah 55:1

5. Isaiah 35:1-2, 30:23, Joel 2:22-27, 3:8, Ezekiel 34:26

6. Isaiah 51:3, 35:1, 29:17

that Jesus' encourages us to invest. He instructs those who will listen with these eternally rewarding words:

> "Do not lay up for yourselves treasures on earth, where moth and rust destroy and where thieves break in and steal; but lay up for yourselves treasures in Heaven, where neither moth nor rust destroys and where thieves do not break in and steal.[1]

Jesus not only makes us aware that we can be rich in Heaven, but He encourages us to focus on it. Investing in the pleasures and comforts of this life will be of no benefit in the next. Instead, He instructs us to fill our treasure chest that is in Heaven.

We could easily scan this thinking it's poetic or even metaphorical language. Many have assumed that this is an analogy for something intangible. However, if Jesus is talking about something intangible, it would be strange to state this principle as He has without letting us know that there is no actual treasure in Heaven. The language points to real treasure that has a physical aspect in the heavenly realm.

Treasure in Heaven is one of the rewards for obedient believers. I'm convinced that when He says "treasure," He means treasure. Considering that there will be a world-wide economy in God's kingdom, I don't see any reason why we need to try to turn this into an analogy.

At one point in the mid 80's when there was talk of market volatility, my grandfather took a large sum of cash and buried it below the dirt of his backyard in a coffee can. When he went to retrieve the paper money a year later, it had utterly rotted in the ground. It had become useless. Now imagine that his financial advisor said to him, "If you bury that money it

---

1. Matthew 6:19-20

will rot-but if you invest that money in gold it will be safe." It would be strange to think that the buried "money" that the financial planner was talking about is a different kind of money than the gold vested "money." It'd be strange to claim that the buried "money" represents actual cash, while the safely gold vested "money" represents something intangible. You would assume that Jesus meant the same thing when he talked about the money in the coffee can as he did when he mentioned the money invested unless he said otherwise. The same seems to be true of Jesus' teaching. From Jesus' words, I don't see a reason to assume that the money invested for the kingdom now wouldn't result in some tangible riches when we arrive in the Kingdom.

He says, "Lay up for yourselves treasures in Heaven, where neither moth nor rust destroys and where thieves do not break in and steal." He teaches us something about the nature of riches in Heaven.

First, notice who you are laying up treasure for. He doesn't say, "Lay up treasure for *God* in Heaven." Instead, He says, "Lay up for *yourselves*…" For yourselves! God doesn't need any more treasure. He's got plenty. In fact, He wants to give it away to His faithful followers. He doesn't just suggest, but He commands you to do things in this life that will result in you having wealth when the kingdom comes. It's treasure that you will own. It will be yours. That's because you've laid it up for yourself.

Secondly, notice in that verse that He doesn't say that treasure in Heaven is something that can't be stolen, but only that there are no thieves in Heaven to steal it. He implies that no one will break in to steal your treasure, that your treasure is safely stored somewhere. He makes it sound as if it's tangible and it's stored at a physical location. The implication is that your treasure will be stored on your heavenly property. This connects to something else Jesus said to His disciples the night He was arrested.

> "In My Father's house are many mansions; if it were not so, I would have told you. I go to prepare a place for you. And if I go and prepare a place for you, I will come again and receive you to Myself; that where I am, there you may be also.[1]

He's promising property to His disciples. His faithful servants will have both treasure and property in which to store the treasure. It's important to see that the word "place" and "Father's house" are both singular. However, "mansions" is plural in the verse. Jesus teaches that there are many individual places for individuals or groups of believers to live in Heaven.

There are even implications that the dwelling arrangements in Heaven will not be evenly distributed among all believers. Jesus said this at the end of one of His parables:

> And I say to you, make friends for yourselves by unrighteous mammon, that when you fail, they may receive you into an everlasting home.[2]

There are everlasting homes. Not only that, but an owner of an everlasting home will be able to "receive" his friend into his home. This is quite natural for us since this is something that friends do all the time in our modern world. If a friend hit a hard time, I'd have no problem letting them crash at my house for a while. If I had a big house, I'd even be happy to have my friends come to live on my estate. So too, there will be property owners in the Kingdom of God. That property will be used to continue relationships with people who you've

1. John 14:1-3
2. Luke 16:9

known on earth, and likely to build new relationships with new friends in the heavenly kingdom.

This verse makes it sound as if there are some who will not receive an everlasting home in the Kingdom, but they will have the option to take up residence with someone who has one. This is also quite natural considering the living arrangements of the original readers of the verse. It was common for one who had wealth and property to take friends into his house as workers. Maybe very faithful believer who is rewarded with a large mansion will be allowed to bring the friends he desires into his house to share in the work Christ has given him. Maybe this is what Jesus is referring to with this statement.

There will be everlasting homeowners, and possibly those who will be given no home in the Kingdom. The ownership of those homes must, therefore, be based on performance in this mortal life.

There is not only treasure stored away in mansions but it will be something carried around and used on a daily basis. Jesus once said:

> Sell what you have and give alms; provide yourselves money bags which do not grow old, a treasure in the heavens that does not fail, where no thief approaches nor moth destroys.[1]

A money bag was a small holder for coins which someone could easily carry for daily purchases. He implies money will be used on a regular and convenient basis. The money bag does not grow old, and the money inside it "treasure" never fails. This makes it sound as if there will be a constant supply of money for those who have been faithful. This money is to be spent, and its regular supply is for those who are doing the

---

1. Luke 12:33

Lord's work. Maybe God's servants will be given an allowance or a stipend with which they can pay for the needs of their daily transactions. This seems to fit with the fact that Jesus allows the faithful servants to keep their earned profits in the parable of the minas and the talents, presumably to be used in their administration over the cities they are given to rule.[1]

Jesus is not passing out treasure and property for free. It's for those who overcome and fight for victory in the Christian life. Note that we don't have any examples of Jesus offering any prime real estate to unfaithful believers. In fact, we have examples of unfaithful believers having their property taken away in the Kingdom.[2] On the other hand, we do discover that faithful believers will be given not only mansions but also cities to manage and rule.[3]

There are even more riches than what is mentioned above, though they will be explored more in a later chapter. The apostles tell us that some unique items of incredible worth will be given to those who live out a victorious life of discipleship. Paul says:

> And everyone who competes for the prize is temperate in all things. Now they do it to obtain a perishable crown, but we for an imperishable crown.[4]

What a cool headpiece you have there. Thanks. It's fashioned by the Lord of Life Himself. The worth of an imperishable crown crafted in the forge of Heaven is impossible to measure. Though if time is money, and our infinite Lord spent even a second making each crown, the worth of these

---

1. Luke 19:11-27, Matthew 25:14-30

2. Luke 19:24

3. Luke 19:17

4. 1 Corinthians 9:25

headpieces would be infinite. Not only will victorious disciples receive imperishable crowns, but some will also receive multiple. More on that later. What goes really great with a fine diadem? Jewelry, of course. Note what Jesus says here:

> "To him who overcomes... I will give him a white stone, and on the stone a new name written which no one knows except him who receives it."[1]

Can you imagine receiving your own custom jewelry with a new name that only you and He knows, from the King of Kings? Some examples of the most famous white gemstones include diamond, sapphire, zircon, topaz, and opal, but there are many more. We don't know if one of these is what the white stone will be made of or not. Maybe different types of stone represent different levels of faithfulness. We're not sure if this jewel will be set in a pendant, or a ring, or mounted within a crown, or possibly even kept hidden. Maybe it is different for each person. Suffice to say that this piece of jewelry which Christ will give to His victors will be uniquely made for its recipient and will be of immense value. The word priceless comes to mind. This will comprise part of the riches possessed by each overcomer. It should be said that the richness of this white stone is not in its monetary worth but in the relationship it represents, but more on that later.

What qualifies someone to be a treasure recipient in Heaven? Jesus laid it out when He said to the rich young ruler:

---

1. Revelation 2:17

"Sell all that you have and distribute to the poor, and you will have treasure in Heaven; and come, follow Me."[1]

Jesus doesn't make it easy; in fact, it's pretty difficult. This young man who loved his wealth was given a difficult task. He could believe in Jesus for salvation and receive it for free, but if he wanted wealth in Heaven, he had his work cut out for him. He was told to sell everything he had and give to the poor. This act of discipleship would gain him treasure in Heaven. Once he'd done this, he was to follow Jesus, which is also an act of discipleship. Salvation is a free gift but gaining treasure in Heaven will cost us dearly. In another place Jesus says to His disciples:

> He who is faithful in what is least is faithful also in much; and he who is unjust in what is least is unjust also in much. Therefore if you have not been faithful in the unrighteous mammon [wealth], who will commit to your trust the true riches? And if you have not been faithful in what is another man's, who will give you what is your own?[2]

There is something very practical about Jesus' instructions. If you were going to set up a world-wide empire and you could pick people to run the finances of the administration, who would you pick? Would you pick people who had a reputation for wasting money on stupid stuff? Or, would you pick people who had a reputation for being very responsible with their money? I know what I would do.

Jesus here teaches that one of the ways in which we will be trusted with "true riches" in Heaven is being responsible with

---

1. Luke 18:22

2. Luke 16:10-12

our money here. Although this includes investment in things that will matter in eternity, the scope seems to be broader than that.

Let's turn the lesson that Jesus gave around into a positive statement. He said, "If you have not been faithful in the unrighteous mammon [wealth], who will commit to your trust the true riches?" If we invert that statement, we get this: "If a believer is faithful in his finances, he can be trusted with true riches." Invest the money you have now in things that matter for eternity, and you will be trusted with true riches in Heaven. Your financial advisor might view giving to a gospel teaching charity as a bad investment, but Jesus is the supreme financial advisor. He expects His committed followers to invest in things that matter for His kingdom.

It's starting to sound like a get-rich program, right? In a manner of speaking, that's what discipleship is. That's precisely why Jesus said discipleship is costly.[1] It's an investment. These riches are not for selfish purposes, instead, they are meant to be used for the glory of God, as are all things in Heaven. That's why He's seeking responsible parties to whom he can trust a fortune. Selfish spenders need not apply.

Toward the end of John's revelation, Jesus says this:

He who overcomes shall inherit all things....[2]

All things! I get excited just writing that. Not only treasure that never fails, true riches, crowns, and custom jewelry, but all things. Certainly, there are untold riches that we have no idea about. Certainly, there are mountains of invaluable things that overcomers will have access to in the Kingdom of Heaven. It's unimaginable.

---

1. Luke 14:25-33

2. Revelation 21:7

Do you want access to these riches? These riches are for those who overcome. Heaven's gold and gems are not for the faint of heart; they're reserved for the one who fights for victory in the Christian life, for those who daily seek the kingdom, and ever conform themselves to the likeness of their coming king. As if this were not enough, next we will explore another facet of reward in Heaven. Not only are there riches, but there are special rights come with being an overcomer. We will see them in the next chapter.

Believers who are **OBEDIENT** on earth will be rewarded with

EXTRA RIGHTS
IN THE KINGDOM OF HEAVEN.

REVELATION 2:7, 3:12, 3:19-20, 22:14

REWARD FOR VICTORY:
RIGHTS

CHAPTER 20

When I was in college my friends and I held a fundraiser for a mission trip. Our campus Christian club got together and drove to Dallas to work for a day at Six Flags Over Texas. For those who live under a rock, Six Flags is one of the greatest places on earth. It's an amusement park. Think Disney Land, but Texas style. I grew up going to Six Flags at least once a year. It was the place of dreams, especially for a kid.

For our fundraiser, we were tasked with running various fair-style games in the kid's section of the park. I had been to Six Flags at least a dozen times, and I was very familiar with the park. At least I thought I was. I had only been to the park as a general access ticket holder. However, being an employee for a day gave me an entirely different view of the place. With our temporary name badges, we were able to go in all of the employee's only locations. This was fascinating to me since I

To view the video for this chapter
GO TO **SIMPLYBELIEF.COM/ER20**
Or scan the QR code with phone camera.

had always wondered what was behind those closed doors. I discovered special employee cafes, four-wheel carts for quick transportation, and secret passageways that allowed workers quick access to rides and attractions. Six Flags was great for people who bought a general admission ticket, but there was even more to see for those who had all-access badges.

Heaven is going to be great for everyone, but there will be special experiences and privileges for those who are given access beyond entrance. There will be an amazing set of rights that overcomers will be entitled to in Heaven. However, before we explore what God's faithful will experience, it's important to learn what rights all believers will have. As you are probably aware, there are certain privileges which He will give as gifts to everyone who has salvation. That means that certain rights are not rewards in the definitive sense. Instead, the rights that every believer has ride along with the free gift of salvation.

In that sense, we may think of these things as the bill of rights for all Kingdom citizens. In fact, citizenship in Heaven is the first right that every Christian will hold for eternity. All believers are entitled to citizenship in the Kingdom of Heaven. We know this because Paul, in speaking to believers who were at various levels of commitment, explained:

> For our citizenship is in Heaven, from which we also eagerly wait for the Savior.[1]

If you've believed in Jesus, then your immigration papers are signed, sealed, and delivered. Your documents await you at the citizenship office of the Heavenly Kingdom. Though we are citizens, it would be inappropriate to live in that country with the flesh we now have. Our lowly, broken and sinful bodies would not be a good fit for our eternal existence in Heaven.

---

1. Philippians 3:20

It's for that reason that Paul doesn't stop at citizenship, but goes on with these words:

> We also eagerly wait for the Savior, the Lord Jesus Christ, who will transform our lowly body that it may be conformed to His glorious body.[1]

So Paul shows us that we will not only have citizenship, but we will gain the right to live out that citizenship in a glorified body. The body will resemble the glorified state of Jesus after His resurrection. The New Testament teaches that this glorified body is not a reward for hard work, but instead a free gift that all believers get for their faith in Christ. Your spirit was reborn at the moment you first believed in Christ.[2] Your body will be resurrected when Christ returns. Your eternal existence will be lived out in a physical body which can do all the things that you currently can do and much more that you can't do now.

Another inalienable right for the saved described in the fourth gospel. John gave us another angle on the salvation of all believers when he demonstrated that each one who believes has the right to be called Children of God. He said it this way:

> But as many as received Him, to them He gave the right to become children of God, to those who believe in His name.[3]

Every person who has believed in Jesus' name has the eternal right to be called the children of God. There will never be a time when they stop being God's child. This right to childhood is not bought by our good works. Instead, this

---

1. Philippians 3:21

2. John 3:3-7

3. John 1:12

special relationship with God was paid for by Jesus' blood. In that sense, it is not a reward but a gift from God.

Jesus gives us another item on the list of the heavenly bill of rights. He explains all believers will have access to the water of life. This is not the only place that talks about the living water which is free for anyone who wants it. Jesus said:

> I will give of the fountain of the water of life freely to him who thirsts.[1]

Notice that there is no caveat or proviso to drinking the water of life. Anyone who has citizenship in Heaven will be able to drink deeply of that cool eternal flow. Although drinking from the fountain of the water of life will be a grand experience, more rights will be offered free to all kingdom citizens. Isaiah gives us a peek behind the curtain of Heaven when he says:

> "Everyone who thirsts, Come to the waters; And you who have no money, Come, buy and eat. Yes, come, buy wine and milk Without money and without price.[2]

Not only the basics of living will be covered but also luxury eating will be available for all kingdom citizens. In the ancient world, the poor might often feed on water and bread, but the rich had a regular diet which included wine and milk. No more will there be people suffering from hunger and thirst in the kingdom of Heaven. Therefore, all kingdom citizens will have the right to eat and drink. No one will starve in that glorious place. Although there are likely a scad more rights which every citizen of Heaven will experience, I hope you see

1. Revelation 21:6-8

2. Isaiah 55:1

the scene.

Although the rights of all saved people are fantastic and enjoyable, there are more rights to which Christ's overcomer will be given access. The rights of the overcomer are greater than the basic rights of Heaven. Heaven will be grand for those who simply believed, but those who also stayed committed through their life will have a greater set of privileges.

Although all Kingdom citizens will have the right to drink and eat, a select group will have the right to dine with Christ. Reference to the right to a seat at Christ's dinner table is found in a number of places. He hinted at it at the last supper when He said to His disciples:

> "I have eagerly desired to eat this Passover with you before I suffer. For I tell you, I will not eat it again until it finds fulfillment in the kingdom of God."[1]

Notice that He compares the feasting He did with His apostles to the feasting that will happen in the kingdom. The Lord's Supper, as we call it, was an intimate setting. The crowds were excluded, and in fact, even many disciples were excluded from this meal. He allowed only His twelve apostles to join Him at this private dinner.[2]

What's amazing is that Jesus indicates this same style Passover dinner will be eaten in the Kingdom. It's astounding to think that this is something that Jesus looks forward to. He likes to sit with His friends and fellowship over a meal. It was something He enjoyed with His apostles, and it is something that He will enjoy with certain kingdom citizens. We find out in another speech of Jesus that not all will be allowed to join Christ at His feasting table. He once said:

---

1. Luke 22:15-16 (NIV)

2. Luke 22:14

I say to you that many will come from the east
and the west, and will take their places at the feast
with Abraham, Isaac, and Jacob in the kingdom of
Heaven. But the subjects of the kingdom will be
thrown outside, into the darkness, where there will
be weeping and gnashing of teeth."[1]

So there will be subjects of the kingdom who are barred
from the feast. The subjects of the kingdom who are cast
out of the feast are saved believers who showed little or no
faithfulness during their lives.[2] Abraham, Isaac, and Jacob,
along with many from all over the world will be allowed to
dine with Christ. Yet, there will be some, possibly many, who
are not allowed this right and privilege. How do we get a seat
at that table? Jesus answers that question in a famous passage:

As many as I love, I rebuke and chasten. Therefore
be zealous and repent. Behold, I stand at the door
and knock. If anyone hears My voice and opens the
door, I will come in to him and dine with him, and
he with Me.[3]

Many have mistaken this passage for an evangelistic one.
However, the context shows that it's clearly talking to saved
believers who have become prideful and distracted from their
walk with Christ. Jesus instructs them, as He instructs all of us.
The right to dine with Christ is reserved for those who listen to
His instruction, respond well to His discipline, and repent of
anything that hinders them from following Him. All believers
will be given the right to dine, but only an overcomer will be

---

1. Matthew 8:10-12 (NIV)

2. We know these are believers because Jesus used the same term to describe saved people in His parables in Matthew 13:38.

3. Revelation 3:19-20

given the right to dine with Christ.

There is more to be said about drinking and eating in the Kingdom of Heaven. Overcomers who are faithful to Christ will be granted the right to eat from the tree of life. Jesus said:

> "To him who overcomes I will give to eat from the tree of life, which is in the midst of the Paradise of God."[1]

It will be a high honor to eat from the tree of life. The fact is, we don't know a whole lot about this amazing tree. In the story of the fall of man, the tree of life was in the garden of Eden. Apparently eating its fruit offered immortality, which was one of the main reasons Adam and Eve were restricted from the garden and the tree.[2]

Not only is the tree of life a fixture at the beginning of the Bible's narrative, but it reappears in the last chapter of the Bible as well. We get this description from John concerning it:

> And he showed me a pure river of water of life, clear as crystal, proceeding from the throne of God and of the Lamb. In the middle of its street, and on either side of the river, was the tree of life, which bore twelve fruits, each tree yielding its fruit every month. The leaves of the tree were for the healing of the nations.[3]

The river of life which all believers will have access to is the water source for the tree. However, this is no normal tree. We find out that it bears fruit in every season and twelve different kinds of fruits at that. The fruit is yielded every month. Also,

---

1. Revelation 2:7

2. Genesis 3:22-24

3. Revelation 22:1-2

the leaves of the tree have some medicinal purposes. The mortal inhabitants of the new earth will be healed by its heavenly foliage. This is a special tree indeed.

The fact that Jesus said, "To him who overcomes I will give to eat from the tree of life," is incredibly exciting. Especially considering that if you and I overcome in our Christian lives, we will be given the fantastic right to eat from this amazing tree. There is plenty of mystery yet to be revealed concerning the tree of life. It suffices to say that this is a privilege we will certainly want.

Just so that we can't mistake what it will take to get this right, Jesus repeats it in the last chapter of the Bible:

> Blessed are those who do His commandments, that
> they may have the right to the tree of life, and may
> enter through the gates into the city.[1]

What will it take to gain the right to eat from the tree of life? It will take obedience. His words, "those who do His commandments," is a reminder that this is a specific privilege for those who are not only saved by faith but also obey Christ in their daily life. In other words, this is not a privilege that all believers will share, but a right of the faithful alone. I can't wait to see that tree and hopefully taste its fruit. What a privilege.

You may have noticed that the above verse offers yet another right that will be available to the overcomer. It says,

> "Blessed *are* those who do His commandments,
> that they may... enter through the gates into the
> city.[2]

The city He's talking about is the New Jerusalem in the

---

1. Revelation 22:14

2. Revelation 22:14

eternal kingdom of Heaven. There will be twelve magnificent gates that remain open at all times. Yet, only overcomers will be allowed to enter the city through these honorable passageways. This hints at a whole system in which overcomers have many special privileges yet to be seen. This does not mean that unfaithful believers will be excluded from entering the city; they simply will not have the honor and privilege of entering the city through the main gates. Surely there will be other, possibly smaller, gates through which the others will enter.[1]

Just as there are certain places in the United States White House where you are not allowed to enter, only overcomers will have the right to enter the heavenly city through these gates. The ancient world had a concept for this in their public parades and triumphal entries of important dignitaries. These twelve gates will be reserved as VIP entrances. How cool that the Lord's overcomers will be the ones who get to use them.

Not only will there be special entrances for the Lord's overcomers, but they will also be given the right to work in the Temple of God. Take a look at how it's phrased here:

> He who overcomes, I will make him a pillar in the temple of My God.[2]

What does it mean to be a pillar? In his letter to the Galatians, Paul called James, Peter, and John "pillars" of the church.[3] The Jewish Rabbis taught that Abraham was the

---

1. Robert Vacendak, "The Revelation of Jesus Christ," in *The Grace New Testament Commentary*, ed. Robert N. Wilkin (Denton, TX: Grace Evangelical Society, 2010), 1333.

2. Revelation 3:12

3. Galatians 2:9

"pillar" of the world.[1] A pillar is a vital part of the structure of an important building. Someone who is made a pillar will be a vital part of the work God accomplishes in the temple. Simpler still, overcomers will be instrumental in doing God's work. The faithful follower of Christ will be given an extremely important occupation that centers on the ever-present work of the Lord. Peter gives us a sense of what that role will be like when he says:

> "But you are a chosen generation, a royal priesthood, a holy nation, His own special people, that you may proclaim the praises of Him who called you out of darkness into His marvelous light."[2]

Not only does being a pillar represent important work done on behalf of the Lord, but it implies an incredible closeness with the Lord as well. Since in the eternal kingdom, there will be no physical temple, but instead, the Father and the Son will be the temple[3] this reward is probably an especially wonderful experience of nearness to God in addition to being a key position of support and prominence in God's eternal kingdom.[4]

This is a reminder that your eternity will not be boring. It's especially true if you are an overcomer because your everlasting life will be packed with important work done directly for the Lord. You will get to work as a vital part of the royal priesthood, proclaiming the story of God to people on the new earth. This is an incredible privilege and right that

1. William Barclay, *The Revelation of John*, 3rd ed. fully rev. and updated., vol. 1, The New Daily Study Bible (Louisville, KY; London: Westminster John Knox Press, 2004), 146.

2. 1 Peter 2:9

3. Revelation 21:22

4. Vacendak, *The Revelation of Jesus Christ*, 1268.

many will wish they had. Though, only those who are faithful will get to experience it.

Although it will be explored more thoroughly in a forthcoming chapter, the overcomer will be given the right to govern the nations with Christ. Jesus will be the High King, and He will appoint overcomers as subordinate kings, judges, counselors, shepherds and likely many other positions that we don't yet know about. To be sure, each position that Christ gives will fit the overcomer's talents and abilities. Although we find many references to this concept, I'd like to share a single verse.

> If we endure, We shall also reign with Him. If we deny Him, He also will deny us.[1]

This simple concept sums up nearly all that we've said so far. If we endure in the faith until the end of our lives; if we work hard and finish well, then we will be given the right to reign with High King Jesus in His royal administration. He will put us in places of authority so that we can do the work that a world-wide kingdom requires. What a privilege that will be.

With this comes a warning, though. He reminds us that if we deny Him, He will also deny us. That is to say, He will deny us the right to reign with Him if we don't continue in the faith. The Bible never says He will deny salvation to a person who believes in Him for it. However, He often says that He will deny us certain rights, one of which is the right to govern if we deny Him in our mortal lives. Becoming heavenly royalty is a right given only to those who prove themselves worthy of the calling.[2] Notice what Paul says only a few words later, though.

---

1. 2 Timothy 2:12

2. Ephesians 4:1

In talking to saved people, he says, "If we are faithless, He remains faithful."[1] Even if a saved person totally fails, Jesus will still remain faithful to His promise of eternal life. Even if a believer is not an overcomer, they will be saved.[2]

We need not ever fear that our salvation could be in question once it's in place. If you have believed in Jesus and have everlasting life, you will have it forever, but if you lean back on that promise and accomplish no good work with your life, the loss will be great when you get to Heaven. The rights demonstrated in this chapter will be available only to the one who overcomes by living a victorious life of faith.

1. 2 Timothy 2:13

2. 1 Corinthians 10:13

Believers who are **OBEDIENT** on earth will be rewarded with
GOD'S RECOGNITION
IN THE KINGDOM OF HEAVEN.

MATTHEW 10:32-33, LUKE 19:17, JOHN 12:26

REWARD FOR VICTORY:
RECOGNITION

CHAPTER 21

Imagine that, after a long and hard career of important work, you get a call from the White House. You are to appear at a ceremony headed by the president. The day comes with all the pomp and circumstance afforded a presidential celebration. As news cameras roll, you shake his hand and humbly receive the verbal praise of the leader of the free world. Though he pins a medal to your lapel, the real prize is his words spoken on your behalf. He talks to the cameras about your many years of selfless service. He relays your achievements to the press core and the gathered audience as you stand by beaming. After wrapping up his speech, he shakes your hand and quietly says in your ear, "I've been following your career for years. You've made a huge difference in the

To view the video for this chapter
GO TO **SIMPLYBELIEF.COM/ER21**
Or scan the QR code with phone camera.

world. Well done!"

Envision for a second how that would feel. What an exhilarating scene. Who wouldn't want such an honor? Who could turn down such an incredible chance to get recognized for his or her work?

No matter how awesome that experience would be, being recognized for your life's work by the creator of the universe will be better by far. There is a day coming when you will stand before the one who stitched the stars into the skies. You will listen as the judge of the heavens assesses your life. He will either give you recognition for your good work, or a reprimand for your poor performance. What a reward it will be to receive His honest compliment. What a crushing blow if he offers words of rebuke.

In the tenth chapter of Matthew, Jesus calls the twelve disciples and appoints them apostles. He gives them the power to cast out demons and heal in His name. After doing this Jesus gives instructions to His newly vested apostles. The chapter is a manual for ministry in the first century. He explains the nature of their future work. Much of what He discusses has to do with the difficulty the disciples will soon face. They will be arrested, tried, and tortured for the sake of Christ. They will be under incredible pressure to be silenced. They will be commanded by judges and governors to stop speaking publicly about Jesus. They will be threatened with death for confessing Jesus as the Christ. He explains to them that the stakes for speaking up about Jesus as the Christ are high. The costs will be great. However, among the instructions, He gives the twelve a motivation to do so. After telling them how difficult it will be, He offers this reward for those who do, along with a consequence for those who won't.

> Therefore whoever confesses Me before men, him I will also confess before My Father who is in

Heaven. But whoever denies Me before men, him I will also deny before My Father who is in Heaven.[1]

This verse is not a call to salvation since it is directed at people who were already saved.[2] It's a call to do one of the fundamental discipleship tasks, confess Christ. Certain actions on earth will have a specific effect in Heaven. A person who confesses before men (on earth) will experience a specific outcome when they arrive in Heaven. Jesus is encouraging all believers to confess Him before men.

A fundamental question we must ask of this verse is, "What does it mean to confess Christ?" Saint Francis reportedly said, "Preach Jesus, and if necessary use words." It sounds clever, but in light of Jesus' teaching on the subject, it doesn't quite cover it.

Jesus explains what confession looks like only a few verses earlier when He says, "Whatever I tell you in the dark, speak in the light; and what you hear in the ear, preach on the housetops."[3] For His disciples, confession happened when they spoke up about what they had learned from Jesus and believed about Him. After all, Paul said, "It is with the mouth

---

1. Matthew 10:32-33

2. These words of Jesus are specifically for believers. There are three reasons we know this. First, the final setting in the verse is Heaven. Notice that both those who confess and those who deny Jesus will be in Heaven. Only believers will be in Heaven, so this verse must be directed only to believers. Secondly, only believers can confess Christ since confession is an expression of one's belief in Jesus. Only after someone believes can they confess. Unbelievers are never instructed to confess Christ since they don't believe in him. The notion is non-sensical. Third, we know these words are directed at believers because Jesus was talking specifically to His twelve apostles. He didn't speak this principle to the unbelieving masses, but to those who were gearing up to do ministry.

3. Matthew 10:27

one confesses..."[1] Jesus said that we must "confess [him] before men."

Therefore, confession is words about Jesus spoken aloud so that others can hear. It's not just any words, though. In the verse, we discover that to confess Christ is the opposite of denying him. Peter denied Jesus three times.[2] Peter's denial was, "I do not know the Man!"[3] Therefore, the inverse would be confession. If Peter had said, "I am a disciple of Jesus, who is the Christ." It would have been a confession of Jesus.

A couple of important verses about confession show up in the Gospel of John. John adds the descriptive help, "...[they] confessed that He was the Christ..."[4] Anyone that declares aloud so that others can hear that Jesus is the Christ (savior) is "confessing." Confession can happen in front of one other person, or a packed room, on a youtube channel, or over the phone. Any time you talk about your faith in Jesus as the Savior, you're doing it. If you've never spoken even privately to a friend about Jesus, it's time.

Now that we know what confession is let's revisit what Jesus says about it:

> Therefore whoever confesses Me before men, him I will also confess before My Father who is in Heaven...

You have a daily decision whether you will confess or not. If you are a faithful servant of Christ, you should be willing to confess your allegiance to him. Fortunately, He doesn't give instructions without giving proper motivation to help us follow

1. Romans 10:10 (ESV)

2. Matthew 26:75

3. Matthew 26:74

4. John 9:22

through. What happens in Heaven to those who publicly confess Jesus on Earth? He says, "him I will also confess before My Father who is in Heaven." Jesus' confession of His faithful servants will happen when they arrive in Heaven. Jesus will give recognition of the bravery and faithfulness of His trusted servants when they enter the kingdom of God.

On your arrival, if you've been obedient, you will get to hear Jesus confess His friendship and pride in you for a job well done. He will talk to His Father and the angels about you. Imagine overhearing Jesus describe you as a friend to His Father. This comprises part of the reward that Christ offers. He will bestow on you the recognition for a high-performance life. What an exciting prospect to be honored publicly by Jesus. Let's take note of the second half of Jesus' phrase.

> Whoever denies Me before men, him I will also deny before My Father who is in Heaven.

The verse doesn't just talk about the good, but also the bad and the ugly. It also says, "but whoever denies Me before men…"

This raises a common question. Is being silent the same as denying Jesus? Let's get some examples of silent believers. There are believers like the cowards in John's gospel who are too afraid to speak up about Jesus. About those cowards John says, "Nevertheless even among the rulers many believed in Him, but because of the Pharisees they did not confess Him, lest they should be put out of the synagogue;" [1] These had saving faith but were afraid to go public with what they believed about Jesus. They would not accept the consequences of confessing, so they stayed quiet.

It's possible to believe in Jesus, and have everlasting life but

---

1. John 12:42

not openly confess Him. It's possible to accept His free gift of everlasting life[1] but not breath a word of it to another living soul. Most of the time, that's not the heart of those who are concerned about this subject.

After reading the first draft of this book, a friend named Jack came to me with concern. He said, "I was talking with an associate the other day about business, and I didn't bring up Jesus. Does that mean I denied Christ?" That may strike you as a familiar concern. It makes many conscientious Christians nervous. When asked, most Christians feel as if they ought to talk about Jesus more often and with more people. However, does that mean that Jack or anyone in this situation has denied Christ simply by not talking about Jesus?

The simple answer is, no. Why? Because if the subject of Jesus had come up Jack would have acknowledged that he's a Christian. Jack is eager to talk to people about Jesus when the opportunity arises. I know this because Jack recently hosted a dinner party where he invited about 100 business colleagues. He asked me to come and share the gospel with those who attended. We worked together to confess Christ to his business associates.

Confessing is about openly acknowledging your faith. Denying is pretending that you have not faith at all. Obviously, there is some space in between. Notice in the verse that Jesus did not say we must confess Christ before all men for Him to be proud of us. Instead, he said before men. As often as the opportunity arises to share Christ, I'm confident Jack will do so. The more we confess Christ, the more proud Jesus will be.

There is no upper limit on how often we should, but there is also no shame in refraining from forcing people to listen to constant awkward talk about Jesus. Some people choose to break the rules of proper conversational etiquette in order

---

1. John 6:47

to chatter about Christ incessantly. I question how effective that is. I'd rather have the kind of talks a conversation partner will enjoy where the subject of faith occasionally comes up, rather than bully a listener into having conversations they are uncomfortable with. I have seen the first method work, and the second method fail time and again. Let's remember that Jesus said only a few verses earlier:

I am sending you out like sheep among wolves. So be as wise as snakes and as harmless as doves.[1]

He's not telling his disciples to bully people into listening to a constant barrage of Jesus jammed jargon. He's saying, like a wise snake who is always watching and waiting, look for opportunities. Like innocent doves, be gentle, respectful, and peace-giving. You're trying to win people over, not force them into conversational submission. People that break the rules of conversational etiquette get listened to but they don't get heard. People who are as wise as snakes and as harmless as doves are constantly looking for an opening, but they don't force their way in.

Sometimes Jesus was silent. Sometimes he had a beverage with his buds. Sometimes he just listened. Though, he was always ready to seize a good opportunity to have a meaningful talk about his Father. We should be the same. Sometimes we listen, talk about the weather, sports, or a new favorite restaurant. Though, we ought to be watchful and ready to talk about Christ. It also doesn't hurt to pray for opportunities.

Now, not all silence is a denial of Jesus. However, there are those who completely refuse to ever speak of their faith even when the subject is brought up. This silent behavior could rightly be called denial. If one goes their entire saved life without ever speaking of Jesus, it's safe to say they have denied Him in this sense.

1. Matthew 10:16

What happens to the cowardly believer who denies Christ? This is where many people trip. Let's tread with caution. Jesus says, "But whoever denies Me before men, him I will also deny before My Father who is in Heaven."

It's easy to think that what Jesus is saying is that the one who denies Him will be denied salvation. We should be careful to notice where this event is taking place. It is happening in Heaven. We established that the person who receives recognition for a job well done is in Heaven when he receives this reward of accolade. Jesus uses the exact same wording to describe the outcome of one who will be denied by Jesus. Therefore, the event at which a believer will be recognized for good work is the same event at which a lazy, cowardly believer will be denied. They are both in Heaven. The faithful saved and the lazy saved are both present in Heaven, but their recognition will be different. The cowardly believer will be denied recognition, he'll be denied the rights mentioned in the previous section, for that matter he'll be denied most of the things mentioned in this book. Being denied by Jesus means, being denied the reward of recognition along with missing out on other rewards.

What will that reception be like? Jesus gives us a clue in His famous parable of the talents. Three servants are given a sum of money to do business. While their master is away two of them perform admirably. On the return of the master, he finds that two of the three are worthy of recognition for their work. To those two faithful servants, he says,

"Well *done*, good and faithful servant; you have been faithful over a few things, I will make you ruler over many things. Enter into the joy of your lord."[1]

Focus on the recognition they receive. As Christians who are taught to be ever humble, we often shy away from admitting that recognition feels good. It's true that seeking fame and renown has littered the path with the wreckage of countless broken lives. Desiring stardom simply for the sake of selfish superiority is a shameful pursuit.

However, seeking the pure acclaim from the one who made us is a lofty goal. Nothing that Christ declares good can be otherwise. If Christ offers this honor as a motivation, then we should not only accept the challenge but relish the opportunity to get recognition from our Lord. It seems Peter had this in mind when he wrote those famous words:

> In this you greatly rejoice, though now for a little while, if need be, you have been grieved by various trials, that the genuineness of your faith, being much more precious than gold that perishes, though it is tested by fire, may be found to praise, honor, and glory at the revelation of Jesus Christ.[2]

Obviously, our eternity will be packed with the sound of our praise and honor to the glory of the Lord. However, God will also do a little praising of His own. We usually think of praise as a one-way street, but Peter pulls back the curtain for us and lets us know that there will be praise, honor, and glory for those whose faith is refined by trials. Not only will we praise and honor Jesus and His Father, but they will also return some of that honor and praise to their faithful servants. The honor bestowed is not from one believer to another, but

---

1. Matthew 25:21-23. Also see Luke 19:17

2. 1 Peter 1:6-7

instead from the creator to His faithfully obedient creation.

My inclination is that the idea that God will praise you for your good service might make some uncomfortable. For most that probably comes from the mistaken notion that praise and worship are the same thing. Your boss may praise you for a job well done, but if he begins to worship you, that would be strange. God will give you some praise if you've been faithful, but He will not worship you. Worship is not a synonym for praise. We need not fret at the idea that God will pour out some praise on his faithful followers. A number of places in the Bible mention this concept. Consider the words of Paul:

> Therefore judge nothing before the time, until the Lord comes, who will both bring to light the hidden things of darkness and reveal the counsels of the hearts. Then each one's praise will come from God.[1]

Notice that last line. For those whose deeds are brought into the light and stand the test, God will praise that person. How fantastic a day it will be when the Lord comes for those who have obeyed him. Jesus adds to this idea when He says:

> If anyone serves Me, let him follow Me; and where I am, there My servant will also be. If anyone serves Me, him My Father will honor.[2]

God will *honor* the one who serves Jesus. This honor will probably manifest itself in many ways, not the least of which will be recognition from God for a job well done. There is no higher honor imaginable than having the God who jumpstarted the spin of the galaxies returning a measure of honor to His servants. The same chapter where this verse

1. 1 Corinthians 4:2-5

2. John 12:26

appears contains this description of a group of believers:

> Many believed in Him, but... they did not confess *Him*... for they loved the praise of men more than the praise of God.[1]

These believers traded in their chance to be praised by God. In exchange, they received the praise of men. They could have confessed Jesus as the Christ, and accepted the consequences that that caused, but they didn't. Instead, they remained silent and counted the praise of other people as more valuable than the praise of God. The praise of God is better than any other praise. Being honored, recognized, and praised by God for our obedience will be an extraordinary experience.

Having my supportive wife tell me "good job" on writing this book is different from getting a great review from a professional literary critic. Getting a thumbs up from a co-worker is very different from receiving a great performance review from a hard-to-please CEO. Getting a commendation for a completed mission from your squad leader is very different from receiving a medal of honor from the President of the United States. Recognition is great, but recognition from the highest office in the land is one in a million kind of feeling.

As awesome of an honor as it would be to get unique personal recognition from the president, how much more phenomenal it would be to get that kind of praise from the Eternal King of Kings. When you stand before Him to give an account of your life, you will be present in a resurrected and sinless body. You will not have even a shade of desire for self-centered praise. You will be able to experience the accolade

---

1. John 12:46-47

from your creator with a pure and noble heart. Although there will likely be millions of memorable moments throughout your eternal existence, this will certainly be one that stands out.

This interpretation may make you uncomfortable. After all, how do we know that this recognition is public? Isn't it possible that Jesus' acclaim for our work will be given in private? Actually, no. Multiple passages tell us our achievements and the resulting reward will be a matter of public record. Remember when Jesus said:

> When you pray, go into your room, and when you have shut your door, pray to your Father who is in the secret place; and your Father who sees in secret will reward you openly.[1]

Give special attention to the last line. In teaching His disciples how to pray, He reminds them of this simple principle. "Your Father who sees in secret will reward you openly." The things that are done humbly in private on Earth will be celebrated in the public banquet halls of Heaven. The quiet acts of a faithful servant will be loudly proclaimed when we stand before our king.

The sublime truth we find in Jesus' words is repeated three times in the same chapter. In addition to the promise about private prayer, Jesus instructs that charitable deeds should be done in private so that God can reward us openly.[2] Fasting, as well, should be done in a way that doesn't bring public attention so that God can reward us publicly.[3] This isn't the only time Jesus gave such promises to put His servants work on public display.

---

1. Matthew 6:6

2. Matthew 6:4

3. Matthew 6:18

> He who overcomes… I will confess his name before
> My Father and before His angels.[1]

The one who lives a victorious Christian life will have a special treat. Notice that Jesus won't just use generic language to refer to all believers, but He will talk to God the Father and the angels about you. He will speak to God the Father about you by name. Imagine overhearing Jesus having a conversation with His Father in which your name comes up. How incredible would that be? It would be nearly impossible to believe if Jesus hadn't told us the truth about it.

Now I know that this is potentially a difficult subject for some. As Christians, humility is so deeply ingrained that it probably makes many uncomfortable to admit that we want that kind of recognition and praise. We are trained to be modest to the point of self-effacing. All that is good while we are here on Earth since our sin nature begs to be let out of its dungeon. If it were left up to egotistical self-gratification, we would chase worldly recognition constantly.

Jesus doesn't deny that there is an innate desire to be recognized for a job well done, He simply reminds us to be patient to receive the kind of recognition that matters. We must be humble now so that our recognition is deferred until we arrive in the Kingdom of Heaven. Don't forget this beautifully simple lesson that Jesus gave.

> For whoever exalts himself will be humbled, and he
> who humbles himself will be exalted."[2]

This is the conundrum in which we find ourselves. We desire the praise of others now. If we pursue praise here, we will be forfeiting the praise of our savior when He is revealed.

---

1. Revelation 3:5

2. Luke 14:11

However, those who see the truth can be motivated to humble themselves here so that they can be exalted there. If it were up to me, I'd be afraid to use the word "exalted." It's a big word. It's a powerful word. It'd raise an eyebrow if it weren't Jesus who said it. He promised that the humble will be exalted.

Notice how He teaches this concept here:

> Therefore, when you do a charitable deed, do not sound a trumpet before you as the hypocrites do in the synagogues and in the streets, that they may have glory from men. Assuredly, I say to you, they have their reward. But when you do a charitable deed, do not let your left hand know what your right hand is doing, that your charitable deed may be in secret; and your Father who sees in secret will Himself reward you openly.[1]

One of the keys to receiving a reward in Heaven is denying reward here on earth. This is especially true of the reward of recognition. If you seek recognition from other people, you will forfeit the recognition reward that Jesus has for those who deserve it. You can either have your reward here or there. Listen to Jesus. He assures us that we would much rather have the reward that Heaven gives than the accolades of earth.

Our charitable work, our prayer, our fasting, our good deeds must be done in such a humble way that it's as if our left-hand doesn't know what our right hand is doing. What matters is the motivation. If what motivates you to volunteer at church is to get recognition from others, then you're going to miss out on the reward for that good deed. The way to ensure that you receive the reward of recognition is first to do good deeds, and second never talk about them. Keep it quiet.

---

1. Matthew 6:2-4

Let your charity be anonymous, and you will be in a good place to receive the reward Jesus offers.

So in our own quiet way, we must wait patiently for the recognition that Jesus will give. Has your spouse failed to notice that you did the dishes? Has your boss refrained from giving you a pat on the back for all the overtime? Has someone else taken credit for your hard work? It stings, but remember that it's Jesus' recognition that we truly want. Stay humble here to receive recognition there.

Believers who are **OBEDIENT** on earth will be rewarded with

REGALIA
IN THE KINGDOM OF HEAVEN.

JAMES 1:12, 2 TIMOTHY 4:8, REVELATION 3:11

REWARD FOR VICTORY:
REGALIA

CHAPTER 22

Regalia includes the insignias and symbols that royalty wear to signify that they are royal. Modern government officials have traded in the traditional attire for the subtlety of business suits and power ties. However, in the old world crowns, signet jewelry, and specific fabrics and color clothing were common regalia of royalty. As we will see in the next section, Christ will appoint overcomers to positions of royalty. Although we will explore that more thoroughly there, it's of value to see what regalia will accompany those positions. What regalia will Christ give His ruling class?

Until the advent of modern fabric technology, one of the most obvious marks of royalty could be seen in the kind of clothes worn. Purple was a popular color for the ruling class since it was expensive to produce and rare. Some of the names of colors still harken back to times when royalty was identified

---

To view the video for this chapter
GO TO **SIMPLYBELIEF.COM/ER22**
Or scan the QR code with phone camera.

by the colors they wore. Royal blue and royal red are examples of this. The average person could not afford to wear these colors, so it distinguished the powerful from the peasant.

In Heaven, the attire worn by the ruling class will also be unique, although the color choice of the Kingdom administration is different from times long ago. Notice what Jesus says about the dress code for the lords and ladies of His royal court:

> You have a few names even in Sardis who have not defiled their garments; and they shall walk with Me in white, for they are worthy. He who overcomes shall be clothed in white garments.[1]

These verses tell us the kind of clothing that overcomers will receive in reward for their faithfulness. Notice that the white garment is given to overcomers who are deemed "worthy." What's of tremendous note is the fact that those who wear white will "walk" with Christ. White robes, as all other rewards, seem to represent a special connection with Jesus. The robes worn will speak of the wearer's faithfulness to Christ for all eternity. It's important to remember, though, that these actual robes are most valuable because of the fellowship with Jesus they represent. On the subject of the white robes in Heaven Dr. Wilkin said this:

> The quality of your eternal garments will be determined by what you do in this life. Once this life

---

1. Revelation 3:4-5

is over, it will be too late to influence your worthiness to walk with Christ in white.[1]

Not only will there be special clothing for those who overcome, but other regal markers indicate who Christ has appointed to His leadership service. We've touched on this verse in a previous section, but now let's look for regalia. Here's what Jesus says:

> He who overcomes… I will write on him the name of My God and the name of the city of My God, the New Jerusalem, which comes down out of Heaven from My God. And I will write on him My new name.[2]

Some believe this "writing" is symbolic. They feel it's unlikely that these will be literal tattoos.[3] Others believe that this writing represents a wearable nameplate like those worn by temple priests.[4] Although these may be true, I see no evidence from the text to indicate that we should not simply take Jesus at His word. He says He will write on His overcomers and I'm convinced that's what He will do. As William Barclay put it:

> In the time to come, when Christ has conquered all, his faithful ones will bear the badge which shows that they are his and share his triumph.[5]

This divine tattoo, so to speak, marks overcomers as

---

1. Robert Wilkin, *The Road to Reward: Living Today in the Light of Tomorrow* (Irving, TX.: Grace Evangelical Society, 2003), 96.

2. Revelation 3:12

3. Vacendak, *The Revelation of Jesus Christ*, 1269.

4. Marvin Richardson Vincent, *Word Studies in the New Testament*, vol. 2 (New York: Charles Scribner's Sons, 1887), 467.

5. Barclay, *The Revelation of John*, 147–148.

belonging to Christ for all time. Just as a tattoo is permanent, so too the divine sort will be more so. Who can wipe off the name which God writes upon the skin of an overcomer? It seems that all overcomers will bear the royal seal, a set of written marks given by the king. These marks will signify the authority which the overcomer has been given, and the relationship he has with Christ. Later in the book of Revelation, we find a group who have already received their divine tattoo at the time when John saw them. John says:

> Then I looked, and behold, a Lamb standing on Mount Zion, and with Him one hundred and forty-four thousand, having His Father's name written on their foreheads.[1]

The writing on the resurrected body of a victorious believer is another reward in the category of regalia. Having the name of God, and the Holy City, and Christ written on the forehead would make it very difficult for anyone to mistake the overcomer for an ordinary person.

The overcomer will be engaged in governing duties throughout the ages of the kingdom. It seems that this mark will remind those he or she leads that the authority comes directly from the king. This regal mark will signify both the relationship which the overcomer has with Christ and the work for which the overcomer has been commissioned.

Probably the best-known rewards of regalia that Christ will give are crowns. Though some believe talk about crowns in the Kingdom of Heaven is symbolic, it's hard to brush away all of the references in the New Testament to being rewarded with crowns. From my quick counting, there are around a dozen references to crowns as rewards. Some of these could

---

1. Revelation 14:1.

be figurative, but it's difficult to believe that this concept is discussed so often if it represents no tangible reality.

Before we dive into what the Bible says about crowns, let's tackle this important question. What is the purpose of a crown?

Historically a crown had more than one use. First, a crown of flowers could be worn at times of joy like weddings and at feasts. Second, a crown was the mark of royalty or authority. Third, the crown of laurel leaves was the victor's prize in sporting games. Fourth, "crown" can be figurative language for an intangible thing like honor, rejoicing, or dignity.[1] The question for the astute Bible student becomes, which of these four meanings is intended when scripture says a crown is offered to victorious Christians? Is it a victor's crown, a crown of royalty, a crown in times of joy, or simply figurative language? I'm convinced that in some cases it might include all.

The crowns which are given specific names in the New Testament are as follows:

1. the crown of rejoicing,
2. the crown of life,
3. the crown of righteousness,
4. the incorruptible crown, and
5. the crown of glory.

These crowns will be given to individuals who overcome in certain ways. Let's look at each in turn. I have organized the crowns in a specific order, with the ones that sound like figurative language first. We will progress toward ones that

---

1. William Barclay, *The Letters of James and Peter*, 3rd ed. fully rev. and updated., The New Daily Study Bible (Louisville, KY; London: Westminster John Knox Press, 2003), 55.

sound much more tangible later in the list.

To start with, Paul makes casual mention of something he calls the crown of rejoicing. He puts it this way:

> For what is our hope, or joy, or crown of rejoicing? Is it not even you in the presence of our Lord Jesus Christ at His coming?[1]

Here we find possibly the best example of "crown" being used as figurative language. He seems to use the word "crown" as a synonym for "hope" and "joy." He then explains that the crown of rejoicing is the people who will be in the presence of the Lord Jesus. The implication is that there will be a great reward with the human capital that Paul has brought into the kingdom.

The reward will be the joy he experiences in seeing his work come to fruition. The reward of souls in Heaven, for Paul, was something he called "the crown of rejoicing." This seems most likely to be figurative language for the emotion he expects to experience when the Kingdom comes. Though it's possible that there will be a tangible crown of rejoicing, I don't think that's what Paul is saying. Nonetheless, we too can experience this figurative crown of rejoicing if we toil at the work of evangelism.

The next crown we will investigate may be figurative language, or it may be a literal crown given out by Jesus. It's called the crown of life. The crown of life is a crown which Christ promises to give to those who persevere through trials and temptations. James says:

> Blessed *is* the man who endures temptation; for when he has been approved, he will receive the

---

1. 1 Thessalonians 2:17

crown of life which the Lord has promised to those who love Him.[1]

Whether or not there is a literal crown of life is hard to say. It's possible that James means a figurative crown made of abundant life. Whatever this crown is, Jesus promised to give it to the one who loves him. This should not be read as an offer for all saved believers. That's because Jesus gave definition to what it means to love Him when He said, "Whoever has My commandments and keeps them is the one who loves Me."[2]

If loving Christ is tied to obedience, then so too must the receiving of this crown. The one who loves Christ by keeping His commandments will get a crown of life. Though this crown may be figurative, I see no reason to reject the notion that there may be a physical crown given that bears this title. Though if that's the case, the crown itself is hardly the reward, the life lived in eternal abundance and fellowship with Christ is the ultimate reward that the crown must represent.

The next reference to crowns uses the title, the crown of righteousness. It is a crown promised to those who love Christ's appearing. These words appear toward the end of what was likely the last letter Paul wrote before his martyrdom. He knew that his death was imminent when he said:

> Finally, there is laid up for me the crown of righteousness, which the Lord, the righteous Judge, will give to me on that Day, and not to me only but also to all who have loved His appearing.[3]

Paul's language here makes it sound like there is a literal crown that is waiting for him. That's because he identifies

---

1. James 1:12

2. John 14:21

3. 2 Timothy 4:8

where this crown is waiting, when it will be given, who will give it, and how he and others earn it. He shows that he will not be the only one who receives this crown, but any believers who "have loved His appearing."

Those who eagerly await Jesus' return and live accordingly will be given this crown. Though it seems to be a literal crown, even if it isn't the implication is clear. Paul is looking forward to what the crown represents.

Though his life was drawing to a close, Paul anticipated being crowned with rulership in the coming Kingdom and the intimacy with Christ that would come along with that. That rulership would be sweet primarily because it would offer him the opportunity to have an eternal working fellowship with the Lord. He invited any who were willing to join him in his eagerness for Christ to return. Those who live in eagerness will receive this crown.

The imperishable crown is also talked about by Paul. The language in this passage also makes it sound as if there is a literal crown to be gained. He says:

> And everyone who competes for the prize is temperate in all things. Now they do it to obtain a perishable crown, but we for an imperishable crown. Therefore I run thus: not with uncertainty. Thus I fight: not as one who beats the air. But I discipline my body and bring it into subjection, lest, when I have preached to others, I myself should become disqualified.[1]

The "crown" that was given to the winner of a foot race in ancient times was made of laurel leaves. We might call it a garland rather than a crown. This is the type of crown

---

1. 1 Corinthians 9:25-27

that Paul compares the heavenly crown to, with one important caveat. Though it was green and beautiful at the time it was given, every laurel head-wreath eventually dried out and perished. Paul compares the perishable victor's crown with the imperishable crown given to those who will overcome in this life. He explains that the one given in Heaven is imperishable. It will never fade away.

He explains how that crown will be earned, as well. He says, "I discipline my body and bring it into subjection, lest, when I have preached to others, I myself should become disqualified." It is going to take hard work as well as a mental and physical disciple to earn a crown which will never fade away. What's more, it's possible to disqualify ourselves from earning this crown. Obviously not being self-disciplined would lose us this heavenly privilege. Once again I must say that the crown itself is not the reason which Paul was striving so hard to earn it. It was what the crown represented that mattered.

The crown of glory is mentioned by Peter and is given to those who demonstrate godly leadership. He puts it this way:

> Shepherd the flock of God which is among you, serving as overseers, not by compulsion but willingly, not for dishonest gain but eagerly; nor as being lords over those entrusted to you, but being examples to the flock; and when the Chief Shepherd appears, you will receive the crown of glory that does not fade away.[1]

We see that Paul was not unique in thinking that a crown will be given to overcomers for a job well done. However, here Peter gets more specific about the group to whom he's speaking. In talking to church leaders, he instructs them to

---

1. 1 Peter 5:2-4

shepherd the flock well with good motives. The crown of glory is one given when Christ, called the Chief Shepherd, appears. This seems to be a specific crown for those who shepherd well. It is for those who offer Christ-like leadership in ministry and Christian community. It's possible that Peter simply uses a different name for the same thing that Paul has already explained, or maybe this is something different. Either way, the case for crowns is beginning to look pretty strong. Peter, James, John, Paul, and Jesus all mention crowns.

In talking to Christians at the church of Smyrna, Jesus said:

> Do not fear any of those things which you are about to suffer… Be faithful until death, and I will give you the crown of life.[1]

So not only do the apostles talk about receiving crowns, but even Jesus mentions His desire to pass out crowns to those who prove worthy of them. Crowns will not be given to everyone at wholesale price, instead, they will be expensive. Jesus says that crown-bearers will have to be faithful until death to get one. Since he's talking to a specific group of people, some of whom were facing martyrdom, He meant this quite literally. He doesn't say that being martyred is the only way to get this crown but instead, "be faithful until death." Not everyone will be martyred, but each has the opportunity to be faithful until death. Not everyone will be victorious in that opportunity. If you continue in faithfulness until your death, you will get a crown. Only a chapter later Jesus says this to another group of Christians in Philadelphia:

---

1. Revelation 2:10

Behold, I am coming quickly! Hold fast what you have, that no one may take your crown.[1]

This comes after Jesus gives them a pat on the back for their hard work in persevering in the faith. He wants them to continue the good work and uses this powerful statement to demonstrate it. "Hold fast what you have, that no one may take your crown," must mean that all believers are able to lose the opportunity to receive a crown, and many likely will. The obvious conclusion is that crowns require perseverance to the end of one's life. Certainly, there are rewards that build up as we go,[2] but from Jesus' words, we see that crowns require that we continue in the faith until we die, even if that death is a martyrdom.

Receiving crowns and other regalia from Christ will be a tremendous experience. However, the bigger picture includes a look at what the regalia represents. The faithful ones will not receive a crown for no reason. There is a very important aspect of Kingdom life to which the crowns will point. That's what we will look at in the next section.

---

1. Revelation 3:11
2. Matthew 6:20

Believers who are **OBEDIENT** on earth will be rewarded with

ROYALTY

IN THE KINGDOM OF HEAVEN.

1 PETER 2:9, REVELATION 2:26, 20:6, 1 CORINTHIANS 6:2-4

REWARD FOR VICTORY:
ROYALTY

CHAPTER 23

It seems that many don't know Jesus' true identity. Sure, they've heard Him called "king," but lots apparently think that is a euphemism, for "a really neat guy." They analogize His title as King of Kings to mean something like, "king of my heart," or "king of spiritual things." Loads seem not to realize that when the Bible talks about Jesus as King, it means it literally. When He returns, He will return with blazing power. He will rule. The angel who appeared to Mary, in talking about Jesus' eternal career, gave this job description:

> He will be great, and will be called the Son of the Highest; and the Lord God will give Him the throne of His father, David. And He will reign over the

To view the video for this chapter
GO TO **SIMPLYBELIEF.COM/ER23**
Or scan the QR code with phone camera.

house of Jacob forever, and of His kingdom there will be no end.[1]

Sounds pretty literal, doesn't it? Although Jesus may be a king in many figurative ways, the Bible presents Him as a literal king who will rule in the hereditary line of King David. That means His throne will be located in Jerusalem, Israel. His rule will last forever. Not only will He rule over Israel but the whole world. In his letter to the Romans Paul explained one of Isaiah's prophecies:

There shall be a root of Jesse; And He who shall rise to reign over the Gentiles, In Him the Gentiles shall hope.[2]

"He will reign over the Gentiles," Paul said. The term gentiles (in the plural) is often used as a designation that means the whole world. Jesus is going to be the King of the whole world. That's not a figure of speech. He's going to have a government administration which He manages from Jerusalem.

It turns out he's not a stingy King who hoards power. Instead, He is interested in giving you a slice of the pie, so to speak. He's looking for worthy servants to manage portions of that world-wide kingdom. He's watching to see if you'd make a good counselor, judge, shepherd, or even king or queen. Even right now, he's considering what job might fit your particular skill set and level of faithfulness. Notice how readily He is willing to share His governance with His servants when He said:

1. Luke 1:32-33

2. Romans 15:12

And he who overcomes, and keeps My works until the end, to him I will give power over the nations.[1]

Who can say stuff like that? Imagine if I went around telling my friends, "If you obey me I'll make you president of the country." They would think I'm nuts. So, either Jesus is crazy to think He can pass out positions of power, or He is going to be king. There is no middle ground here.

Jesus said that He would give power over the nations to those who obey. If you are faithful to him, He will remember your faithfulness when He begins to pass out posts in His government system. By the way, this is no new idea. The prophets had been talking about this opportunity for centuries before Jesus arrived. There are lots of examples, but my favorite comes from Daniel. He said:

But the saints of the Most High shall receive the kingdom, and possess the kingdom forever, even forever and ever.'[2]

Daniel points out that the saints (that's us) will possess the kingdom forever. The implication seems to be that once Jesus appoints His ruling class, they will always be His ruling class. There is a permanence to the kingdom arrangement. That's one of the reasons it matters so much that you get with the program. If you play loose with your Christian life, you may be missing out on a tremendous opportunity not just for a little while, but for all eternity.

In Revelation, there is a song that will be sung in Heaven. A verse of it goes like this:

---

1. Revelation 2:26

2. Daniel 7:18

231

> For You were slain, And have redeemed us to God
> by Your blood Out of every tribe and tongue and
> people and nation, And have made us kings and
> priests to our God; And we shall reign on the earth.[1]

What a fantastic praise and worship song. Notice that one of the things that the Lord is being praised for is "making us kings and priests" and allowing us to "reign on the earth." His work was not only to give salvation but so that those who receive salvation would be made into priests and kings.

In the Old Testament, priests could only be from the tribe of Levi. However, here we find out that God will use people from every tribe and tongue for His class of priestly rulers. Peter adds to this idea by telling us a little bit about what the career of a royal priest will look like when he says:

> But you are… a royal priesthood, a holy nation,
> His own special people, that you may proclaim the
> praises of Him….[2]

The royal position that faithful believers will have will not be for the ego-bloating of the royal priest. The purpose is to glorify God. The work that Jesus' royal class will engage in will be a job of God-honoring duties.

Wanting to be among the ruling class is not a self-centered aspiration. If you think it is, it's probably because so many earthly kings have been so bad. Instead, in the Kingdom Jesus will appoint people to positions of priestly rule so that they can honor, praise, and worship God through their work. They will, likewise, be leading the inhabitants of the earth to do the same. What an amazing job. I can't wait!

Paul gave us another indication to what it will take to be

1. Revelation 5:9-10

2. 1 Peter 2:9

appointed to this royal priestly vocation when he said:

> For if we died with *Him,* We shall also live with *Him.*
> If we endure, We shall also reign with *Him.*[1]

Once again we see the common thread of endurance. Short-lived enthusiasm won't do it. A spiritual sprinter is not the one for whom Jesus is watching. He's looking for someone who can run the marathon and not faint. Like a skill-eyed coach, he's assessing His servant's commitment to the long distance race. Certainly, some rewards will be "laid up" for those who demonstrate isolated stints of faithfulness.[2] However, rulership in the order of the heavenly priesthood is not a job for the faint-hearted.

We get a sense of what kind of attributes He values in His royal priests from words spoken during His ministry. Most forget the context of the verse I'm about to show you. Jesus was explaining what heavenly rulership would be like when He said:

> You know that the rulers of the Gentiles lord it over them, and those who are great exercise authority over them. Yet it shall not be so among you; but whoever desires to become great among you, let him be your servant.[3]

The mother of two of the disciples had just asked Jesus to appoint her sons to high royal positions in the kingdom of God. He was explaining that rulership in the Kingdom won't look like the rule of human kings of the past. Instead, servant leadership is critical. Those who desire authority to "lord it

---

1. 2 Timothy 2:12

2. Matthew 6:20

3. Matthew 20:24-26

over" others are not suited for this job. This is an occupation for those who understand what it means to be a servant. In a more concise statement Jesus put it this way in another place:

> Blessed are the meek, For they shall inherit the earth.[1]

Do you want to inherit the earth? If your answer is "Yes," then be careful. If you want to inherit the earth to exercise power over other people, you probably are not acting meekly. Sometimes the best leaders are the ones who don't desire to lead. In this case, Jesus is judging who He will put in charge of portions of His kingdom based on meekness. Those who will take the attitude of a servant may well hear these words of Jesus when they enter the kingdom of God:

> 'Well done, good servant; because you were faithful in a very little, have authority over ten cities.'[2]

What a powerful thought that Jesus will decide whether you are suited for being heavenly royalty based on your actions now. So consider this a job interview, the longest job interview of your life. In fact, the job interview is your life.

As with most things, it's easy to get the focus off of Jesus. This is especially true when we start talking about our destiny as Heaven's royal authorities. The thing to remember is what the true reward is. Though it's a beautiful reward to reign with Christ, reigning without Christ would not be a reward at all. It's Jesus and our proximity to Him that makes the reward worth having.

All believers will be "with Christ" throughout eternity.[3]

---

1. Matthew 5:5

2. Luke 19:17

3. 1 Thessalonians 4:14

However, the higher the position a resurrected believer is appointed to, the closer he or she will be to the King of Kings, Jesus. There will be those who performed so poorly during their life that they will be blocked from some of the privileges shared by faithful believers.[1] Others will receive a partial reward and a lower position.[2] For these there will be waiting a kind of middle management role,[3] so to speak. Jesus reveals that there are even positions at His right hand and at His left hand.[4]

The greatest reward will not be the job we are given, but the closeness that job affords us to the boss. Though all saved people will have a satisfying relationship with the Lord throughout eternity, those at the right hand and left hand of Jesus will have much more interaction and contact with Him than those in middle management, or lower.

A lot of people seem to panic when they consider existing forever. Add to that the idea propagated by popular culture that our cloud-sitting eternal existence might be a bit boring. Anyone who thinks Heaven will be boring has failed to see the incredible satisfaction that heavenly work will afford the worker.

Let's imagine you're looking for a job. You start by looking for local, "now hiring" signs. When you finally find an opening, what's the first thing you want to know about that potential job opportunity? You probably want to know the size of the paycheck. We've spent pages talking about that. So what's the next thing you want to know about a job opening? You want to see the job description.

---

1. Matthew 8:11-12

2. 2 John 1:8

3. Luke 19:18-19 shows a servant who does moderately well and is not commended for his excellent work and is given only a partial reward.

4. Matthew 20:20-23

As it turns out, we have a description for the job of Christ's co-rulers. Though we have to piece it together, since it appears all through the Bible. Let's find out what Heaven's royalty will be doing with all that time we are going to have on our hands. The job is probably not like what you're thinking.

There will likely be much more to the job than we know, but a common thread runs through descriptions of the kingdom of Heaven. Scripture mentions a time when God will restore righteous leaders and counselors. Isaiah reports God's words thus:

> I will restore your leaders as in days of old, And your
> counselors as at the beginning. Afterward, you shall
> be called the city of righteousness, the faithful city.[1]

This verse is talking about a time that hasn't happened yet. It's talking about the future kingdom of Heaven on earth. God says that He will once again put people in places of leadership and counselorship who guide the people as God desires. He compares them to the days of David's rule[2] when David followed after the heart of God and led the people accordingly. This is a big part of the job description for those who will be royalty in the Kingdom of God. They will be leaders and counselors.

It's worth noticing that the verse doesn't say, "I will restore a leader and a counselor." Instead, it says that there will be many leaders and counselors. Being a leader of people in the kingdom of Heaven will not be a lonely job. There will

---

1. Isaiah 1:26. The first line is taken from the NIV and the second from the NKJV. I've used a mix because I believe it demonstrates the translation better.

2. John A. Martin, "Isaiah," in *The Bible Knowledge Commentary: An Exposition of the Scriptures*, ed. J. F. Walvoord and R. B. Zuck, vol. 1 (Wheaton, IL: Victor Books, 1985), 1037.

be many others who are working alongside you. Jesus always sent His disciples out in groups of at least two. Leading and counseling will be teamwork. What sweetens the deal is that the team you get to work with is one that you love perfectly. There will be no interoffice squabbles or managerial power plays. Instead, your team of glorified leaders will have a single-minded unity as they drive toward the goal.

And what of the goal? Notice also that the leaders and counselors get the work done. They don't toil in vain, endlessly fighting against incredible suffering only to end their tenure to find that there is still insufferable cruelty throughout their domain. The verse says that after these leaders and counselors are restored, the city will be called "the city of righteousness." In other words, these leaders and counselors get results. Their governing works, which is not what we see in the world today.

It's written into our DNA to want to help others. Though our sinful flesh gets in the way, we have an innate desire to teach those who want knowledge, to encourage those who need confidence, and to enrich those who have questions with answers. Think of the times you've helped someone, and they have deeply appreciated it. Didn't that make you feel great? Now imagine that being your job. Counseling, and leading people toward a greater and more fulfilling life. I can't imagine anything more satisfying.

Let me pause here to say that if leading, ruling, and reigning sounds scary or difficult to you then you're not alone. Being in charge of a company of strong-willed people will turn your hair grey. Being in charge of a country of sinful citizens will shorten your life, sometimes by firing squad. Governing is the hardest job there is, and it seems that only the foolish are willing to do it. In fact, I've had many people reply after a discussion about ruling with Christ that it doesn't sound all that great.

They're not alone. Many think this, but they think this because they imagine what it would be like to rule over sinful, fallen people. However, the verse we are about to look at gives us a peek into how it will be different to rule and lead in the kingdom. I hope you will begin to reconsider your trepidation as you look at what Isaiah said about the job description in this beautiful statement:

> I will also make your officers peace And your magistrates righteousness. Violence shall no longer be heard in your land, Neither wasting nor destruction within your borders; But you shall call your walls Salvation And your gates Praise.[1]

These verses point to a time when Heaven will finally be on earth.[2] Governing in the future kingdom will not be the toilsome laborious job it is today. The job will be pleasing because peace and righteousness are the governing forces that drive the population. In the kingdom, people will be committed to these lofty ideals. Imagine offering direction and governorship to a group of people who are sinless. It would be a different task than governing today's thick-headed, stiff-necked people.

Jeremiah sweetens the job description when he says:

> At that time they will call Jerusalem The Throne of the Lord, and all nations will gather in Jerusalem to

---

1. Isaiah 60:17

2. Earl D. Radmacher, Ronald Barclay Allen, and H. Wayne House, *Nelson's New Illustrated Bible Commentary* (Nashville: T. Nelson Publishers, 1999), 869–870.

honor the name of the Lord. No longer will they follow the stubbornness of their evil hearts.[1]

People who act like that would be a joy to lead and guide. In fact, I get excited just thinking about the kind of shared eagerness that the world's inhabitants will manifest toward worshiping and learning about God. In that same section, Jeremiah gives us another look at the job description for the King's faithful followers. He says:

Then I will give you shepherds after my own heart, who will lead you with knowledge and understanding.[2]

Isn't it cool to think that Jeremiah was talking about you if you endure when he mentions these godly shepherds? God will give the people leaders who guide them like gentle shepherds. They will be led into knowledge and understanding of God. Imagine being the teacher of the most eager-to-learn, respectful, and obedient class ever imagined in the history of education. They hang on every word. They hope the lesson never ends. They beg you for an encore. That is what reigning in the kingdom of Heaven will be like. It's not about pushing the little guy around; it's about feeding the hungry minds and hearts of a people who have a passion to learn more about God.

Paul talked about our eternal job description when he said:

And God raised us up with Christ and seated us with him in the heavenly realms in Christ Jesus, in order that in the coming ages he might show the

---

1. Jeremiah 3:17

2. Jeremiah 3:15

incomparable riches of his grace, expressed in his kindness to us in Christ Jesus.[1]

We are an eternal object lesson, a class of redeemed teachers who can speak first hand about God's mercy and grace. In the "coming ages" He will use us to show how rich in grace He is. We often forget that God has an eternal purpose for saving us that goes beyond our own enjoyment. He is planning to use us for this specific job throughout the ages. As we counsel, shepherd, and teach, we will be fulfilling His plan to bring Him fame through our own story and descriptions of what he's done for us.

I can imagine the enthralled faces of sinless future inhabitants of the kingdom of Heaven. They will marvel at your description of what the world once was. They will gasp at the stories you tell about what God did in the ages past. They will celebrate at your description of what God has done for you and them. The work of sharing the knowledge of God which you've gained and been given will be a never-ending journey of satisfaction.

Although we looked at an abbreviated copy of this verse a few pages ago, it's worth repeating in its entirety. Peter explained the job description with these words:

> But you are a chosen generation, a royal priesthood,
> a holy nation, His own special people, that you may
> proclaim the praises of Him who called you out of
> darkness into His marvelous light;[2]

Though we proclaim His praises in this life, this verse will have a fuller fulfillment in the kingdom of Heaven when it finally comes to earth. The royal redeemed will speak publicly

---

1. Ephesians 2:6-7

2. 1 Peter 2:9

and privately about the God who gave so much to call them out of the darkness into brilliant light. They will lead the flock with stories about their powerful experience that echoes back through dark times. They will guide and counsel faithful sinless people with their worshipful words.

Being royal, having authority over the nations, being a counselor, or a shepherd is probably not quite what you had imagined at the beginning of this chapter. The job will be incredible and infinitely satisfying. It's a job that will take meekness to accomplish. It's a job of service. It's a job of sacrifice. It's a job that we will love doing down through the ages. Yet, its greatest satisfaction will come from the relationships it offers us; relationships with others; but more importantly, our relationship with the one whom we will be praising. We will discover more about that in the next chapter.

Believers who are **OBEDIENT** on earth will be rewarded with

A CLOSER
RELATIONSHIP
WITH GOD IN THE KINGDOM OF HEAVEN.

GENESIS 15:1, REVELATION 2:27-29, 22:16 2:17 3:19-21

REWARD FOR VICTORY:
RELATIONSHIP

CHAPTER 24

Imagine that at the end of your life you show up in Heaven. You receive a bevy of rewards for your hard work. However, at the end of the rewards ceremony, what if God says, "I've decided to separate you from myself for eternity, but you can keep all of these rewards I have given you." How would you feel? I'm glad it's only in our imagination because that would be the most crushing blow I can imagine. If it weren't for our relationship with God and Christ, none of the other rewards that He offers would matter at all. That's why the reward we are going to look at in this section, ties all the others together. Without the reward of a closer relationship, no other reward would even be a reward.

So far we've seen that victorious disciples will be rewarded with riches, recognition, rights, regalia, and royalty. Now we

To view the video for this chapter
GO TO **SIMPLYBELIEF.COM/ER24**
Or scan the QR code with phone camera.

come to the big one. Without the aspect we are about to see, all the other types of rewards would be truly meaningless. The previous six aspects of Christ's reward would be nothing but an empty shell if it weren't for this one thing. What is it? We call it relationship.

The final and foremost aspect of eternal reward is the quality of our relationship with Christ and with God. Did you know that not all believers are promised the same closeness of relationship with the Lord? Let's see what the Bible has to say about this.

Every believer will have a relationship with God. Also, all believers have a relationship with Christ forever. That's why John said:

> But as many as received Him, to them He gave the right to become children of God, to those who believe in His name:[1]

No saved person will be left entirely out of a relationship with the Lord. Everyone to whom Christ gives eternal life will be included in this state of childhood forever. Once a child always a child. You could think of this in biological terms. Once you're physically born, you will always carry the DNA of your parents. Whether you have a good relationship with them or not doesn't change the fact that you will always be their child. In this aspect being a child of God is similar. Once you're born into the family of God, you will always be in the family of God. You will always have a relationship with Him.

It's exciting to think about what will come after this life for all believers. Jesus gave us a glimpse into the hereafter when He said to His disciples:

---

1. John 1:12

I will come again and receive you to Myself;
that where I am, there you may be also.[1]

Have a child of God relationship means that the believer
will always be "present" with Christ. He promises that those
who have eternal life are guaranteed to spend their eternity
with him. Although the capacity which will be fulfilled by each
believer may vary, one thing is assured. If you have believed
in Jesus for everlasting life, you will spend that life with him.
That's why Paul could confidently say:

> Then we who are alive and remain shall be caught
> up together with them in the clouds to meet the
> Lord in the air. And thus we shall always be with
> the Lord.[2]

In talking about what we've come to call "the rapture,"
Paul indicates that every person who has been born again,
regardless of their performance, will always be with the Lord.
This will be accomplished in the endless years that follow that
special event.

Although we could spend much more time on the promises
given to all believers, it's valuable to move to what all believers
will not have in common. Though each saved person will have
a relationship with the Lord, some will have a more rewarding
relationship than others. This might, at first, surprise you to
find out that the Bible doesn't offer an equal eternal experience
for all eternally living believers. In fact, the Bible draws a line
between those who have been faithful and those who have not.

The greatest reward on Earth and especially in Heaven is
Relationship. Intimate fellowship with Christ, the Holy Spirit,
and God is the thing to be sought above all. On hearing that

---

1. John 14:3

2. 1 Thessalonians 4:17

statement, some people might be concerned, thinking that I'm talking about some emotional experience with God. Too often we've made feelings the metric by which we judge our relationship with the Father, rather than looking at the criteria that the Bible gives us. So if this kind of discussion concerns you, don't worry, it will be made plain and simple by the verses we will look at in this section.

The first thing to understand is what constitutes intimacy with Christ. I recently received a question from one of my readers who said she *didn't feel the presence of God* anymore and was concerned that there was something wrong. I brought her attention to what the scripture says about having a close relationship with Christ, which is what I will do with you as well. The first statement I'd like you to see comes from Jesus' own mouth. He said to His disciples:

> You are My friends if you do whatever I command you.[1]

It's so important to see that intimate fellowship with Christ has to do with obedience. Those who rely heavily on having an emotional extravaganza for proof of closeness with God may well miss this point. To be a friend, and I'll say a *good* friend of Jesus, requires obedience to what He taught. Regardless of how you feel, if you refuse to obey the teachings of Christ, you're no friend. You can be a child of God and yet be a rebellious child. You can be saved but not act as a friend of Christ. The quality of your relationship is connected to obedience to the Lord.

Now with that said, let's look at the reward of relationship. What is the greatest reward you could receive? If you've got your wits about you, you'd answer with the plainest Sunday

1. John 15:14

school answer there ever was: God is the greatest reward there is. To be in His presence, and to experience all that He wishes to allow us to experience through relationship with him. In fact, the scriptures indicate this early in the Bible.

> The word of the Lord came to Abram in a vision, saying, "Do not be afraid, Abram. I am your shield, your exceedingly great reward."[1]

Notice what God calls himself here. Among other things, God names himself Abram's exceedingly great reward. Do you want to have an exceedingly great reward? I do. No reward is more excellent than God. But what does it mean? How can we receive God as a reward? Through relationship.

Did you know that Abraham was called, "a friend of God." Not only in Judaism, but in Christianity, and in the Islamic faith as well. Abraham became known as God's friend. This friendship is a fantastic example of him receiving the exceedingly great reward, that is God.

Those who balk at the notion that we should be motivated by eternal rewards which will be given out in Heaven have likely missed this point. The greatest reward is relationship with God and by proxy, Jesus. Without this, no other reward is even a reward at all. Riches, recognition, rights, regalia, and royalty would be empty without a relationship with God. It's the relationship with Him that will allow us to experience fulfillment for all of eternity.

Overcomers will have a closer relationship to Jesus than those who didn't obey. There will be those who have a more fulfilling relationship than others in Heaven. That's why this subject matter is of an eternal importance. The intensity of your relationship with God in Heaven will to a large extent be

---

1. Genesis 15:1

determined by your faithfulness during this life. The quality of your relationship then will depend on the quality of your obedience now. Remember what Jesus said in Revelation:

> Behold, I stand at the door and knock. If anyone hears My voice and opens the door, I will come in to him and dine with him, and he with Me.[1]

Jesus offers himself as a reward for those who live a godly life. He pictures for us an intimate dinner at which we can either leave Him standing outside as He knocks, or let Him in. For those who are willing to let Him in, the reward will be great. The exceedingly great reward will be to share an intimate fellowship with him.

Notice that He gives conditions for this. He doesn't offer it to just any who believe. It's not for all believers. Instead, He says in the previous verse:

> As many as I love, I rebuke and chasten. Therefore be zealous and repent.[2]

Responding well to Christ's discipline, repenting of shameful deeds, and accepting the lifestyle that goes along with these things are the requirements to experience this kind of intimacy with the Lord. It's hard to imagine how intensely we will desire to have this closeness when we arrive in the Kingdom of Heaven. We will want to be close to Him more than we will want any other thing. However, at that time, it will be too late to change how we lived on the Earth. That's why we must work hard toward this opportunity.

Jesus adds to the concept of an intimate dinner with these words:

---

1. Revelation 3:20
2. Revelation 3:19

> To him who overcomes I will grant to sit with Me
> on My throne, as I also overcame and sat down with
> My Father on His throne.[1]

Not only will there be the kind of closeness that comes from eating together, but also we will get to work together. What will Jesus' job be in the Kingdom of Heaven? He will be ruling from His throne. That's an important occupation. What He reveals here is that those who seek after the reward of relationship with Him will not only get to spend leisure time with him but also work time as well.

My closest friends are those with whom I both play and work. My wife is a good example. Our intimacy is never stronger than when we get to work together on projects that we love. It's a beautiful concept to imagine that some will get to spend that kind of quality time with the King of Kings.

In these words, Jesus gives us an indication of the type of intimacy that overcomer will share with him. He says, "I will grant to [the overcomer to]sit with Me on My throne, as I also overcame and sat down with My Father on His throne." Notice that He compares our opportunity to share His throne with His opportunity to share His Father's throne. He seems to be implying that we can have a similar kind of relationship to him, as He has with His Father. That's incredible even to write those words. Imagine the intimacy that the overcomer will be able to experience as they share the chair of power with the King of Kings. This is an exceedingly great reward.

There is something practical in His words. One might ask how sharing His throne could equate to intimacy. The reasoning is apparent when we understand how the Kingdom hierarchy will work. His faithful servants will be rewarded with responsibility and opportunity in the Kingdom of Heaven.

---

1. Revelation 3:21

Those who receive more authority will have a closer relationship with him. This is similar to the way that the president's cabinet of top advisors has constant access to him, whereas a low-level intern may only have brief interactions. The practicality of sharing Christ's throne seems to be a promise of interactive fellowship born out by Kingdom accomplishment.

But wait, there's more. Take a look at this statement from Jesus toward the end of the book of Revelation:

> I am the Root and the Offspring of David, the Bright and Morning Star.[1]

Jesus calls himself the morning star. The morning star that we see in the sky is Venus. It's extremely bright and circles the sun in a tight crown-like pattern. It rises brilliantly before the morning's first sunbeams. It's sometimes called the herald of the dawn for this reason. When the morning star crests the early horizon, you know that soon the day will follow. Jesus was a star that rose out of Israel[2] to herald the dawning of a new age. He was long awaited, eagerly anticipated, and is the gift of God to the world.[3] He is given to all men and women for salvation by faith alone, but He will be given in a special and unique way to those who overcome. Jesus says:

> He who overcomes, and keeps My works until the end... I will give him the morning star.[4]

This alludes to an extraordinary kind of relationship which will be shared between Jesus and those who fight for the victory in their mortal lives. This offer stands for any willing

1. Revelation 22:16
2. Numbers 24:17
3. John 3:16
4. Revelation 2:26, 28

to suffer through the pain of a life lived for God. It's not a gift for everyone who believes, but instead a reward for fulfilling a specific condition. What's the condition?

One must overcome, and keep His works until the end. It will be hard work, but the reward will be worth it. The Joy and satisfaction that will be experienced by those who share the Morning Star will be unmatched by those who do not have this privilege.

One of the more enigmatic promises of scripture appears in the same book. Revelation reveals a great number of the rewards that Jesus intends to give. The ones mentioned in this verse are as mysterious as any, but there are some clues as to what they mean. See what else Jesus promises to give to overcomers:

> "To him who overcomes I will give some of the hidden manna to eat. And I will give him a white stone, and on the stone, a new name written which no one knows except him who receives it."[1]

At first glance, these promises seem mysterious, but there is little doubt that the original audience would have quickly understood since the ideas are rooted in their culture. For the overcomer, Jesus first promises a portion of the hidden manna, not only to look at but to eat. What is this hidden manna all about?

God fed the Israelites in the desert with a kind of bread that came down from the sky.[2] He also instructed them to take an omer of manna and keep it in the ark of the covenant.[3] It was to remind Israel how God had provided for them in

---

1. Revelation 2:17
2. Exodus 16:14-15, 31
3. Exodus 16:33

the wilderness. However, the original ark of the covenant was permanently lost in 586 b.c.[1] And the manna inside had vanished before then. Jewish tradition claimed that Jeremiah[2] had hidden the ark and that it would be restored at the end time.[3] This information still does not answer the questions that Jesus' words raise. Will Jesus give us literal manna, or is this a metaphor for something else?

Remember what Jesus said to the hungry crowd near the Sea of Galilee. The previous day He had fed around five thousand of them. This really intense conversation follows in which the people are trying to pressure Jesus into more miracles. To Him, they said, "Our fathers ate the manna in the desert; as it is written, 'He gave them bread from Heaven to eat.'"[4] The conversation continues, but Jesus refuses to give them what they want. Instead, He reveals something profound about himself. In fact, He repeats it many times.

In the 6th chapter of John, the word "bread" is used 17 times. Jesus uses the word 11 times to describe himself. Here are a few:

Vs. 33 For the bread of God is He who comes down from Heaven and gives life to the world.

Vs. 35 I am the bread of life. He who comes to Me shall never hunger, and he who believes in Me shall never thirst.

Vs. 48 I am the bread of life.

---

1. Jeremiah 3:16
2. 2 Maccabees, 4 Baruch claim that they were hidden by Jeremiah. 2 Baruch claims it was an angel that hid them.
3. Craig S. Keener, *The IVP Bible Background Commentary: New Testament* (Downers Grove, IL: InterVarsity Press, 1993), Re 2:17.
4. John 6:31

Vs. 50 This is the bread which comes down from Heaven, that one may eat of it and not die.

Vs. 51 I am the living bread which came down from Heaven. If anyone eats of this bread, he will live forever; and the bread that I shall give is My flesh, which I shall give for the life of the world."

Vs. 58 This is the bread which came down from Heaven—not as your fathers ate the manna, and are dead. He who eats this bread will live forever."[1]

Over and over Jesus repeats these same words. It's almost comical how many times He has to say it. Each time, the Jewish audience seemed to resist it a little more. They just weren't getting the message, so He continued to try to drill it into their heads. Jesus tells us about a dozen times in one chapter that He is the manna. He makes it extremely clear that the manna is a representation of what He offers and not the other way around.

As if that were not enough, Luke records Jesus' words and actions at the last supper. "And He took bread, gave thanks and broke it, and gave it to them, saying, 'This is My body which is given for you; do this in remembrance of Me.'[2] Not only does Jesus invite His disciples to eat the bread which represents His body, but He instructs them to do it on a regular basis. This is an image of Jesus offering himself for us. However, there seems to be something it will represent in the Kingdom of Heaven.

---

1. John 6:33, 35, 48, 50, 51, 58
2. Luke 22:19-20

Now let's return to the promise of Christ, which we are investigating. He said, "To him who overcomes I will give some of the hidden manna to eat." What did we learn in John six and Luke twenty-two? We learned that Jesus is the manna. Jesus is the manna. Jesus is the manna. I won't repeat it 11 times as Jesus did, but remember Jesus said it over and over so that we wouldn't miss the point.

So Jesus is the manna, but is He hidden? About being hidden, Jesus said, "I shall be with you a little while longer, and *then* I go to Him who sent Me. You will seek Me and not find *Me*, and where I am you cannot come." Jesus[1] identified Himself as being both manna and being hidden. In every way possible, Jesus represents the hidden manna.

If Jesus is the hidden manna, what does that mean for those who are allowed to eat it? Although we only have a key-hole view of this promise, we can surmise that it has something to do with intimacy with our Lord. The one who lives out a victorious Christian life will be given exclusive access to Jesus, the manna that was hidden for so long. The overcomer will be allowed a kind of experience with their Lord, the Bread of Life.

I'm convinced that there is some connection to Jesus' words, "Man shall not live by bread alone, but by every word that proceeds from the mouth of God."[2] For the overcomer feeding on the hidden manna might mean gaining sustenance from the words of God. Maybe it means that the words spoken by Christ will directly sustain overcomers. Whatever the case may be, it will be an experience that not all believers will have.

This is not the only promise given in these verses. Let's review what He said:

---

1. John 7:33-34
2. Matthew 4:4

> "To him who overcomes I will give some of the hidden manna to eat. And I will give him a white stone, and on the stone a new name written which no one knows except him who receives *it*."[1]

We've unraveled the mystery of the hidden manna, but what is the meaning of the white stone? Many have proposed ideas to explain this enigmatic statement. There is so little information given that I have to admit I don't know. With that being said, I have a pet theory that seems most reasonable to me.

I am convinced that the white stone is a reference to a new kind of Urim. Never heard of that? That's fine. I'll explain. In the Old Testament, the temple priests were to keep two small stones in their chest pocket, one white and one black. The stones, called the Urim, and the Thummim were to allow the priest to cast lots to know God's decision on any given matter.[2] You can think of the Urim as something similar to drawing straws or tossing divine dice. The Urim would be used to find out what God wanted the people to do. This was very important in cases where a hard decision needed to be made. *Urim* is the Hebrew word for "lights" and therefore would logically be associated with bright or white stones.[3]

If this assessment is right, the white stone Christ will give to His champions is a symbol of intimacy with Himself and with God. It seems that the overcomer who receives this stone receives with it access to the inner will and desire of God. The overcomer will have a kind of fellowship with the Lord that not everyone will share. He won't have to wonder from a

1. Revelation 2:17

2. Exodus 28:30, Numbers 27:21

3. Victor Harold Matthews, Mark W. Chavalas, and John H. Walton, *The IVP Bible Background Commentary: Old Testament*, electronic ed. (Downers Grove, IL: InterVarsity Press, 2000), Ex 28:30.

distance what God thinks. He will have a means by which he can learn the desires of the Lord.

In another reference to a unique intimacy with the Lord, Jesus promises that there will be "on the stone a new name written which no one knows except him who receives *it*." In Jesus' earthly ministry, He liked to give out nicknames. He called Simon, "The Rock," and the Zebedee brothers, "Sons of Thunder." He called Nathaniel, "A True Israelite." Imagine receiving your own unique name from the Lord who made you. We know precious little about what these names will be, but we know they will be unique and special.

Ultimately, this stone represents a personal connection between the recipient and the giver. Jesus will share some inside knowledge with each overcomer. This hints at the kind of fellowship that the Lord offers to His champions. It's not the kind of relationship that a celebrity gives to his fans, but instead the sort of fellowship a friend offers a friend. How Jesus can share this kind of connection with every champion, must rely on His divine nature. Rest assured, that those who have this relationship with the Lord will be incredibly fulfilled. Those who miss out on this are missing out on the opportunity of eternal closeness with the one who gives ultimate joy.

Only a chapter later He gives this promise, which is hard even to fathom:

> He who overcomes, I will make him a pillar in the temple of My God, and he shall go out no more. I will write on him the name of My God and the name of the city of My God, the New Jerusalem, which comes down out of Heaven from My God. And *I will write on him* My new name.[1]

We've seen in a previous section what it means to be a

---

1. Revelation 3:12

pillar in the temple of God. The focus, I'd like to point us to in this section is the fellowship that this will offer. Imagine the kind of closeness one would experience with God being instrumental in the activities of the temple. What's more, in the eternal kingdom, there won't be a temple building because the Lord God Almighty and the Lamb are the temple.[1]

Notice the next line where He says, "and he shall go out no more." In the Jewish temple, there was a special place called the Holy of Holies. Only the high priest could enter it, and only for a short time. This was the place where God was most present. By saying, he will go out no more," Jesus is telling us that the overcomer will never leave the presence of the Lord. The temple had outer courts and inner courts, but to enter the holy of holies was a special honor. To get to stay in the holy of holies is an honor that no human has ever experienced. Though, for the champions, God will extend this honor in the kingdom of Heaven. This likely doesn't mean that they will physically stay in one place, but instead that anywhere they go, they carry the palpable presence of the Lord with them. Overcomers will be traveling tabernacles who carry the presence of God with them throughout the kingdom. No matter where an overcomer goes, they never leave the company of the Lord.

The greatest reward that anyone will ever experience in eternity is a maximally intimate relationship with God. The closer someone is to God, the more joy and fulfillment they will experience. As we've seen in this section, not everyone will have an equal relationship with the Almighty and Christ when the Kingdom comes. Some will have a closer fellowship with God than others. We should strive to live in a way now that prepares us for the greatest kingdom experience. The greatest reward in all eternity is a closer relationship with the Lord.

---

1. Revelation 21:22

CONCLUSION

In this study, we've covered a significant number of things concerning eternal rewards. I know it is cliche; but even after writing forty three thousand words on this subject, I still feel like there is a mountain to say about eternal rewards. After all, they are an aspect of our future experience that we will enjoy forever. There is always more to say about anything that will last forever. I'm sure when we arrive in the kingdom of Heaven we will discover we knew so little it's laughable. I'm glad, however, that we know enough to be motivated toward good works. I hope what you've seen in this book will guide you as you continue to look into this exciting and essential topic.

If you have enjoyed this book, please feel free to contact me. I'm a click away. You can reach me through our team's website simplybelief.com. You can also find me @lucaskitchen on the major social media networks. We would love to discuss this further or set you up with other resources and materials. If you're interested in a live appearance, let me know. I'd love to come and talk with your group, congregation, or conference. We're excited to share this and other important messages with believers.

Thank you so much for reading.
-Lucas Kitchen.

SELECTED
BIBLIOGRAPHY

Barclay, William. *The Gospel of Luke, The New Daily Study Bible* (Louisville, KY; London: Westminster John Knox Press, 2001)

Barclay, William. *The Letters of James and Peter,* 3rd ed. fully rev. and updated., The New Daily Study Bible (Louisville, KY; London: Westminster John Knox Press, 2003)

Barclay, William. *The Revelation of John,* 3rd ed. fully rev. and updated., vol. 1, The New Daily Study Bible (Louisville, KY; London: Westminster John Knox Press, 2004)

Hodges, Zane C. *Faith In His Name: Listening To The Gospel Of John.* (Corinth, TX: Grace Evangelical Society, 2015)

Hodges, Zane C. *Romans: Deliverance from Wrath*, ed. Robert N. Wilkin (Corinth, TX: Grace Evangelical Society, 2013)

Hodges, Zane C. *The Epistle of John: Walking in the Light of God's Love* (Irving, TX: Grace Evangelical Society, 1999)

Keener, Craig S. *The IVP Bible Background Commentary: New Testament* (Downers Grove, IL: InterVarsity Press, 1993)

Kitchen, Lucas. *Salvation and Discipleship: Is There A Difference.* (Longview, TX: 289 DESIGN, 2016).

Martin, John A. *"Isaiah,"* in The Bible Knowledge Commentary ed. J. F. Walvoord and R. B. Zuck, vol. 1 (Wheaton, IL: Victor Books, 1985)

Matthews, Victor H. Mark W. Chavalas, and John H. Walton, *The IVP Bible Background Commentary: Old Testament,* electronic ed. (Downers Grove, IL: InterVarsity Press, 2000)

Radmacher, Earl D. Ronald Barclay Allen, and H. Wayne House, *Nelson's New Illustrated Bible Commentary* (Nashville: T. Nelson Publishers, 1999)

Strong, James. *A Concise Dictionary of the Words in the Greek Testament and The Hebrew Bible* (Bellingham, WA: Logos Bible Software, 2009)

Swanson, James. *Dictionary of Biblical Languages with Semantic Domains: Greek* (New Testament) (Oak Harbor: Logos Research Systems, Inc., 1997)

Vacendak, Robert. *"The Revelation of Jesus Christ,"* in *The Grace New Testament Commentary,* ed. Robert N. Wilkin (Denton, TX: Grace Evangelical Society, 2010)

Valdés, Alberto S. *"The Gospel according to Luke,"* in *The Grace New Testament Commentary,* ed. Robert N. Wilkin (Denton, TX: Grace Evangelical Society, 2010)

Vincent, Marvin R. *Word Studies in the New Testament, vol. 2* (New York: Charles Scribner's Sons, 1887)

Wilkin, Robert. *The Road to Reward: Living Today in the Light of Tomorrow* (Irving, TX.: Grace Evangelical Society, 2003)

SCRIPTURE INDEX

John

John (continued)

Acts

Romans

1 Corinthians

2 Corinthians

Revelation (continued)